THE PROS AND THE CON

THE TRUE STORY OF TWO NY CITY DETECTIVES
THAT BECAME LEGENDS
UNDER THE STREET NAMES
OF BACKSTAGE AND SOFT-SHOES

TED FARACE
WITH ANDY CAMERA

THE PROS AND THE CON

During the 70's, the city of New York was plagued by street con artists committing swindles with losses exceeding a million dollars. The Queens confidence team consisting of NY City Detectives Ted Farace known as Backstage and Andy Camera known as Soft-Shoes, was formed to combat these crimes. At first, their focus was the borough of Queens and later encompassed the entire city of New York.

This is the true story of how Ted and Andy's ingenuity and creativity helped reduce the number of crimes dramatically. The street names were created and used as a psychological tool to instill fear into the criminals that they will be found and prosecuted. Their reputation spread to other states, creating a legacy that still exists today.

Major cases were solved with the help of their confidential informant. She furnished critical, valuable information on wanted criminals. This information led to their arrests for multiple swindles after years on the run. Our Informant contacted Detective Ted Farace, Backstage, after 50 years and was instrumental in motivating him to write this true story.

The Pros and the Con

First edition — January 2025

Published in the United States of America
This edition published by IngramSpark

Cataloging-in-Publication Data has been applied for.
Book cover design by Lisa Ceraso-Farace

ISBN: 979-8-89778-354-0

www.theprosandthecon.com

CONTENTS

INTRODUCTION

ACKNOWLEDGMENTS

THE START

THE BEGINNING DAYS

Chapter 1   Intelligence Gathering and Birth
               of Backstage & Soft-Shoes

Chapter 2   What Are Confidence Games

Chapter 3   The Informant

Chapter 4   Conned the Con

Chapter 5   Surveillance Pays Off

Chapter 6   Awareness and Training

Chapter 7   Phony TV Sale- Manhattan DA's Squad

Chapter 8   "Drag" Solo Player

Chapter 9   The Gypsy Swindle

Chapter 10   Barbara St. James Investigation

Chapter 11   News Stories and Images

Chapter 12   Conclusion/Summary

INTRODUCTION

This is the true story of two New York City Detectives, Ted Farace and Andrew Camera, and their careers as "Bunco Rollers" investigating the street hustlers committing crimes what was known as confidence games.

The 1970s was a violent time for the citizens of New York and other major cities across the country. Crime was up on every level, homicides, robberies, burglaries, and confidence games. The Pigeon Drop, Handkerchief Switch, Phony TV, and Gypsy Swindles were common street hustles in New York City during those years, known as the confidence games. In the world of confidence operators, Ted and Andy were better known by their street names, Backstage and Soft-Shoes from 1972 to1979.

Adding to their seven years of success, they were joined by a confidential Informant who had participated in confidence games, nationwide. This Informant furnished information that led to the arrests of individuals wanted for major crimes.

The Informant, reconnected with Detective Ted Farace, "Back-stage" in 2024 after losing contact for almost 50 years. She rekindled the desire in contributing to this book and was one of the main characters that inspired the publication of this true story.

ACKNOWLEDGMENTS

This book is dedicated to all the law enforcement officers who investigate known confidence games across this country. Especially Detective Jon Grow of the Baltimore Maryland Police Department for his inspiration in co-founding the National Association of Bunco Investigators (NABI). Jon passed away in 2012, he will be missed. His efforts have saved so many seniors from losing their money and entire life savings.

I would like to express my gratitude to my daughter, Suzanne Ferrufino, for her exceptional editing and guidance throughout the process of bringing this book to life. Thank you for helping to shape this work into something I am proud to share with readers.

I would like to extend my sincere thanks to my daughter-in-law, Lisa Farace, for creating the stunning cover design for this book. Your creativity and vision have truly brought the essence of the story to life, and I am grateful for your talent and dedication.

The input from our Informant was invaluable. Her detailed explanation of her life prior and during her time as a Drag girl added so much value to this true story.

I would also like to thank my wife, Laura Farace whose patience, understanding, and constant support have meant the world to me throughout the entire process of authoring this true story. Writing this book has been a labor of love, but it also came with its share of challenges. Laura's encouragement and belief in me kept me grounded and motivated, even when the journey seemed overwhelming.

THE START

Detective Theodore Farace

In the spring of 1964, I, having graduated from high school and not wanting to attend college, joined a major financial institution on Wall Street. I was placed in the stock transfer department handling securities daily. After work, a group of young men and myself from the securities department played softball in a bank league. The team practiced at Central Park in New York City. One of the players, Carl Benson (pseudonym) wanted to be a New York City Police Officer. At the time, he was attending Delahanty Institute to train for the written exam for the police department. He would go two or three times a night to attend classes. Back in the early sixties, the exam for becoming a Police Officer was difficult unlike today's exam to join the force. Applicants back then had to pay a fee to take this exam.

The New York City Police Department was under enormous stress to recruit qualified candidates to fill open positions because of retirements. The city decided to open the exam as a free walk-in test for anyone interested in becoming a New York City Police Officer. One Saturday in late July, Carl took the exam for this position. The entire softball team, including myself, went to the facility to support Carl and took the exam. We did not expect to pass because we did not study like Carl. This was just a sign of support for our friend. At the time, I was married and had one young son. I had no interest in becoming a police officer with no relevant knowledge of what the job entailed, unlike Carl who had family members in the police department. The exam lasted about 1.5 hours. After we all went to Central Park and played a few games of softball. At the practice, Carl was extremely excited and felt he had done well on the exam and was looking forward to the results. The rest of us shrugged off this feeling being we were not interested in a career as a police officer.

Weeks later, I received a letter from the City of New York, as did some of the other members of the softball team. To my surprise, I passed this exam with a score of 78 and other members of the team did as well. Now the decision had to be made on whether I take this job or turn it down. Carl was so excited he had passed and was looking forward to joining the department. He encouraged me to consider taking the job and explained the benefits, medical, pension, and decent salary at the time. At the time, college was not a prerequisite as it is today to join the New York City Police Department. The only other requirement was taking a physical and medical exam. There were also height requirements, 5'8" minimum to join. I was 6' so no issue for me. Carl on the other hand was close to 5'8" and might have an issue. Carl had convinced me to take the job and after discussions with my wife, I decided to take it. In addition, having passed the exam, five other members also took the job. A couple of them would drop out after a few months of training but a couple did make it through along with Carl and myself. Carl had been seeing a chiropractor to help him stretch so he would make the 5'8" requirement. On the day of the medical exam, we went to his home and carried him out on a piece of plywood, while he was stretched out to make the 5'8" height requirement. We carried him into the facility on the plywood and he just passed the height requirement. After that, we all went out for a couple of beers to celebrate.

On August 17, 1964, I was appointed as a New York City Police Officer as were Carl and the others. After 6 months of training and physical education, we graduated and were assigned to various police precincts. Carl was assigned to the 1st Precinct in Lower Manhattan (he lived on Staten Island), and I was assigned to the 69th Precinct in Brooklyn. The police department at the time tried to assign you as close to home as possible. The others were assigned across the city. Over time, I was the only one that stayed connected with Carl. My first days at the 69th Precinct were a revelation. I was assigned foot patrol and really did not like this. The precinct was quiet regarding crime, except in the north end of the precinct, which bordered East New York where crime was extremely high.

After months on foot patrol, I finally was placed in a marked patrol car which gave me more exposure to arrest situations and police work than on foot. The NYPD had a career path that an officer had to take to become a detective dealing with narcotics and public morals assignments, and then possibly to the Detective Division and a Gold Shield. For me, I wanted no part of those units and remained on patrol in a sector car.

In early 1968, the then Chief of Detectives made a decision to open opportunities for patrol officers to advance to becoming a detective without going through the other units in the career path program. He asked each precinct to submit one name of an officer for consideration. I was chosen based on my arrest record. There were over one hundred precincts and each person selected (over one hundred) had to go before a review board at police headquarters for consideration to advance to detective. I arrived at police headquarters, at that time in Lower Manhattan on Center Street, and joined one hundred or so candidates for the detective division. After sitting in a hallway for the entire day, I was the last candidate to go before the review board. The board consisted of three Chiefs, which were high-ranking officers. They focused more on my arrest record, which was quite good. One Chief said to me, "I think we can find room for you." Weeks later, I was assigned to the Brooklyn South Detective Task Force with three other partners all chosen from the one hundred submitted. We were asked to go out and affect arrests, which we did. We had the highest arrest record of all the teams formed and were promoted as probationary detectives still working with the white shield. My team was broken up based on our last name and our assignments in alphabetical order. I was assigned to Brooklyn North, the 80th Detective Squad in Bedford Stuyvesant area of Brooklyn. I worked in that squad for six months and was given my Gold Shield as were my three detective partners. I worked at the 80th Precinct for close to three years. In 1972 when Specialization started, I was transferred to the 16th Burglary Larceny Squad working out of the 103rd Precinct in Jamaica, Queens. That precinct is what started my career in the investigation of Confidence Games, using the street name "Backstage."

Detective Andy Camera

In the fall of 1952, Andy graduated from high school and joined the Long Island Press, a major newspaper in Long Island and Queens, New York. He became a copy boy, the term used by reporters and advertising people to pick up written information from companies. This information was called copy and artwork, used to prepare for future newspapers. During that time, Andy was drafted into the Army at the end of the Korean War. His assignment was in Panama due to unrest regarding ownership of the Panama Canal. Andy was assigned to the Infantry at Fort Kobbe. During prior years, he always thought of becoming a police officer. In Fort Kobbe, Andy was given permission from his captain to switch from the Infantry to the 544th Military Police Unit. After completing his military service, Andy returned to the newspaper business and stayed there for a couple of years. In 1956, passed the New York City Police Officers exam and was appointed in November 1957. His first assignment was in the 103rd Police Precinct in Jamaica,

Queens. After years on foot patrol in that precinct Andy was assigned to a marked radio car. This precinct was the most prone area in all of Queens for high crime. He was fortunate having a good partner to work with for close to four years, and as a result developed a good arrest record. As a result of his record, in 1964, Andy was assigned to the Youth Squad as a career path to becoming a Detective and receiving the Gold Shield. This squad dealt with youth crimes, gang street crime and underage drinking. Two years later, Andy received a promotion to detective and received his Gold Shield.

Having been promoted he was transferred to the 80th Precinct Detective Unit in Bedford Stuyvesant in Brooklyn, New York. Andy was lucky to have another good partner for five years investigating all types of crimes, from homicides, robberies, burglaries, and assaults. In 1971, he was promoted to second grade detective, again, based on his arrest record. During the time spent in the 80th Precinct Andy was going to John Jay School of Criminal Justice in New York City under the G.I. Bill for education. He received a Bachelor of Science degree and went on the obtain his master's degree in Public Administration. Specialization came to the New York City Police Department in 1972, and as a result Andy like Ted was transferred to the Queen Burglary-Larceny Squad, located in his old command the 103rd Precinct. Working in the Queens Burglary Squad alongside Ted Farace who had also worked in the 80th Detective Squad back in Brooklyn years earlier were chosen to investigate known confidence games. This was another new career for Andy as "Soft-Shoes."

THE BEGINNING

The Detective Division of the New York City Police Department undertook a dramatic reorganization in 1972. Detective Squads were replaced by specialized units working in burglary, robbery, sex crimes and homicide. Confidence games formerly were managed by precinct detective squads which were thrown into the newly organized Burglary Squads citywide. The tremendous monetary loss sustained by the schemes were never fully realized in the past, since each precinct detective squad managed a specific number of crimes which were never reviewed on a New York City borough wide command level. However, it quickly became a problem of major consequence when all the schemes reported are now managed by the newly formed Queens Burglary Squad.

The Queens district commander decided he would pick two detectives from the newly formed Burglary Squad who would be willing to learn how confidence games are perpetrated and affect arrests. Only six arrests had been made in the Borough of Queens in 1971, for confidence games, while the monetary loss was over $500,000. Certain expertise was needed by these detectives in the complete understanding of confidence schemes. There were certain major ruses that were given top priority such as the Pocketbook Drop or Pigeon Drop, Handkerchief Switch, Phony TV sale, Gypsy Blessing crimes, and Spanish Confidence games. The two detectives selected were Detective Andy Camera and myself whose street record for arrests in the Burglary Squad were rated number one and two. The District Commander's instructions were incisive, if only for its brevity. He told us, "Go out and make collars (arrests). Make your own hours, just give me 40 hours a week." We found ourselves out on the street, without a vehicle and only with a cursory knowledge of confidence games. Limited knowledge had been gained from discussions with the 16th Burglary Squad Sergeant, who formerly had been assigned the city-wide Pickpocket Confidence Squad located in Police Headquarters. Additional knowledge came from scanning reports of confidence games successfully complied in our squad. We had the most valuable tool to manage our new assignment, which was made up for the lack of knowledge and equipment this early stage of our assignment, which was a burning desire to succeed. It was agreed by us that we would fare much better on foot than using an unmarked detective unit. At the time, a detective vehicle was easy to spot. Any 12-year-old would know it was the police. A high number of confidence games were committed in the 103rd precinct on Jamaica Avenue. This area was our focus to start. The other members of the 16th Burglary squad expressed surprise that we would attempt to tackle these types of schemes without a vehicle, but they respected us as detectives, with jokes resulting about our new career. Since our office was located in Jamaica, Queens an area that was of high incident of the schemes; we set out on foot, feeling highly motivated.

After breaking off, each taking one side of Jamaica Avenue, we started our tour. We were not sure what exactly we had to look for, but as seasoned detectives that was not a problem. After approximately two hours of looking at everybody in sight, we saw several females in conversation with an elderly female. We remembered from the sergeant who had worked in the Pickpocket Confidence Squad that the phony money used in this ruse will be in a pocketbook of the confidence women. Since we were not sure if we had our first collars (arrests), we immediately called for backup and took everyone into the precinct to be investigated. We left the suspects in our interrogation room watching them through the two-way mirror, hoping they might open their pocketbooks to get rid of the phony money.

After a while we realized we had made a mistake. They were not a confidence team but innocent bystanders. We sure wanted to pack this detail in right there. Eventually, both girls were released when we checked out their story further. We found out they had a job interview scheduled in the area and our detainment of them messed up their opportunity for the job. Luckily, they were good sports and took the detainment in stride. It was then we both realized this detail is a little more difficult than we thought. We vowed to be more careful before jumping the gun in the future. Little did we know the future was only 15 minutes away! As we were cementing our relationship with the two girls by driving them to the subway at Parsons Blvd in a borrowed detective's vehicle, my partner and I observed men across from the subway entrance in conversation with a female. I said, "They look good."

In retrospect, this was my first inkling that I was made for this work. I was not only driving the car, and talking to the women, but also scanning the street for con-operators at the same time. This pattern was to continue throughout our confidence game career, which spanned seven years. We practically pushed the two women out of the car and jumped out to follow the two men on foot. Meanwhile the person who was speaking to the two men was heading down the subway stairs to board a train. I went down into the subway to approach the female (victim) to find out what had transpired. Andy kept his eyes on the two men. They entered a car driven by a female and were about to leave the area. I came back up from the subway and gave Andy a thumbs up signal. That meant the story given to me by the female victim was she had been conned. We approach the car they were sitting in and took them into custody. All we could think about to ourselves was that we hoped we were right this time. As we investigated the car, we saw a handkerchief rolled up laying on the floor with what looked like money inside. We then knew we had our first collar, and it felt good.

Andy and I worked for a period of years in the highly volatile Bedford Stuyvesant area as precinct detectives before coming to the Queens area and into this new assignment. During those years we had both built up impressive arrest records in managing all types of crimes, from homicide to petit larceny. Yet somehow, these confidence arrests gave us a tremendous kick, unlike that of any of the previous arrests we made during our careers. Andy and I took our prisoners up the stairs to the Burglary Squad office, detectives were coming down and they asked the usual question, "What's you got?" When we answered them, that it was a couple of con operators, one of the detectives shouted back "A couple of what?" It naturally was a term not often cited in the past. The District Commander was informed that day about the collars we made. The Commander was extremely happy and remarked to us," That's what I call fast work." It then hit us that it had only been three hours since we had left the office with the statement of "Getting some collars." We thought to ourselves that this assignment might prove remarkably interesting.

As we were processing the two prisoners, an off-handed remark was made by one of the prisoners referring to one of the subjects as "Skinny." He did not know his real name but knew his street name. It was our first clue to the importance of street names as a means of identification in the confidence circles. It later proved invaluable as an investigative tool and more important, intelligence information gathering.

Four more arrests following in quick order during this same month, all affected while we were still on foot. The other members of the 16th Burglary Squad were kidding that we had more arrests on foot than the rest of the squad who were assigned department autos. However, the full extent of the confidence game problems was quickly being realized in the borough of Queens, as increasingly completed schemes were reported to the police. The Commanding Officer of our unit contacted the Pickpocket Confidence Squad at headquarters to request additional help to deal with the ever-growing problem. However, the Pickpocket Confidence Squad had the entire city to deal with, over one hundred precincts, so the problem Queens was considered was minimal in comparison to the larger boroughs of Brooklyn, Bronx, and Manhattan. Even so, the Pickpocket Confidence Squad responded by sending one of its senior detectives as the best officer to train both Andy and I. He would collaborate with us in the field and teach us the ropes.

The assigned Detective George, a first-grade in rank and it immediately become apparent to us that Detective George really knew his business; having worked in this squad for over ten years. His reputation as a tough detective only strengthened our interest in collaborating with him. Unmarked detective vehicles, free from distinctive markings, were still a problem in the initial stages of the detective reorganization (Specialization). Detective George volunteered, although reluctantly, to use his own vehicle for our street surveillance. There was no way he intended to waste time looking for 'Drag' (Pocketbook Drop) females or 'Stuff' (Handkerchief Switch) players on foot. Detective George insisted that if we really intended to make it in this business, we had to start thinking like street people. Therefore, our homework assignment for the next few days included words never uttered in any English class: 'Drag' was the term or street name for the Pocketbook Drop; 'Jug,' referring to a bank; 'Lame' or 'Mark,' a victim; 'Hit female,' a female who found the pack with money; 'Pack,' an envelope with large amounts of cash; 'Catch female,' a Drag female who engages a victim in conversation; 'Stuff,' the street name or term used for the Handkerchief Switch game; and 'Michigan Roll' or 'Mish,' a roll of fake money with a real bill on the outside.

It was our first contact with the street jargon used in con games by both players and detectives known as the Bunco Rollers, who are knowledgeable in the various schemes. The Drag girls are those who played the Pocketbook Drop or Pigeon Drop con game. The first Drag female would stop the victim—called the Vic, Mom, Mark or Lame—and engage in conversation. The female was called the Catch. The second female, the Drag girl, that enters the conversation is called the Hit Girl since her approach involved showing the Vic, Mom, Mark or Lame the found envelope called the Pack, which allegedly contained a hefty sum on money. We learned quickly and never again to refer to confidence operators in such banal terms as con girls and con men. Detective George knew we were a willing audience to his helpful tips, and he rose to the occasion. His reputed aloof and authoritative personality never really surfaced in his short two weeks with us, he was willing to teach us the inner workings of the various confidence schemes. We quickly realized that our knowledge to date, bolstered by our quick street success was severely limited. We listened intensely to everything Detective George had to say, realizing that if we were truly to excel in this field our opportunity was at hand. One statement by Detective George, though innocently absorbed by us at the time, came back to reveal itself throughout our career, "You will know it when you see it" replied Detective George in repeated questions by us about the ability to spot those Drag girls and Stuff players on the street. If we had to settle on one major point in instructing other detectives in confidence game expertise, we would emphasis that rather simple and encompassing statement. Detectives who really gain the necessary expertise in confidence surveillance work can spot a team while they are riding through an area looking for the right Lame. A great deal of street knowledge and exhausting surveillance is required for this elevated level of expertise, but we found it proved repeatedly worthwhile.

The weather was brutally warm during this July spell and foot surveillance was preferred by us, but Detective George wanted to cover a greater area of the borough of Queens which could only be accomplished in his vehicle. Detective George remarked that Drag girls do not play one area, but ride looking for the right Lame. We thought we were going to have comfortable tours of duty in Detective George's car until we found out his air conditioning did not work. The mornings were not too hot, but the afternoons were brutal. In surveillance work of this type, you must continually eyeball the street and sidewalks as well as observe cars passing by. Such surveillance work is particularly demanding by its constant and concentrated attention to the surroundings around you. There is only a brief second to analyze a passing car or person(s) on the street and form an opinion. Delay in forming an immediate decision might result losing the car and a team. Experience was later to show us that often we tailed cars and spotted people on the street we thought looked good only to find out after minutes that we did not have a confidence team.

After about a week of exhausting surveillance in Detective George's vehicle, we began to feel that this supposed high incidents of the Pocketbook Drop or Pigeon Drop confidence schemes were over exaggerated. We realized seven arrests had been made while on foot surveillance and confined to the Jamaica, Queens area. Now, we broadened our surveillance area to include a larger portion of the borough of Queens, as the highly respected Detective George was instructing us, still we had not spotted a team in over a week. George could tell we were becoming a little restless and quickly reminded us that patience is necessary in this type of assignment. He no sooner had the words out of his mouth when he yelled to Andy, who was driving the car, "Stop." Andy taken in by the suddenness of Detective George's direction and the fact that George started to sink to the floor "When I say stop, I mean STOP." Andy jammed on the breaks, as Detective George said, "Do not let them see me, they might know me." Andy made a U-turn and chased the vehicle Detective George saw;

however, the car was out of sight. Detective George cursed the slowness of Andy's response to his command, showing the famed, but previously hidden, authoritative personality of Detective George.

Things never were quite the same after Detective George's outburst. We began to realize the importance of quick maneuverability and a fast gas pedal in dealing with these types of crimes. We also realized that we needed a big arrest to offset our loss of that apparent team. Surprisingly, we were rewarded the next day. The following morning, we were all still upset over losing the collars the day before. Andy was again behind the wheel, determined to do better this day. Detective George occupied the passenger's side, and I was seated in the rear. We had learned from our radio car days that scanning both sides of the street increase mental fatigue thus hampering our observational abilities. Therefore, to maximize our efforts, Detective George concentrated on the right side of the street, and I on the left side of the street with Andy upfront. After two hours of surveillance, a 1969 Chevrolet with New Jersey tags pulled out from a side street onto Parson Blvd in Jamaica. We noticed it had one female occupant, the driver, and it struck us that she seemed over cautious in her driving. She kept her left directionals on even though she was quite a distance from the next main intersection with cars in front of her. We decided to keep her under observation, and she proceeded to make two complete turns around the block. Detective George stated," We have a team" again using that familiar statement, "You will know it when you see it." His statement concurred with the feelings that Andy and I had already formed. She kept looking all around while she was driving, so we dropped back to give her room. On the third turn around the block she parked her car at a meter and waited. We pulled into a nearby parking lot and watched from inside our vehicle. Detective George started to duck down again in the seat as he did on the previous day. He stated, "She might recognize me." Andy and I began to wonder whether this was an act by Detective George to impress us or whether the veteran detective had attained that level of notoriety in the confidence world requiring such anonymity. Suddenly a second female appeared by her car and entered to join the driver. She bent down inside the car and appeared to be putting something together. Detective George exclaimed, "They have a Lame on the hook, and they are preparing the Mish, the roll of fake money." Detective George continued to speak, telling us they must be playing with a third partner who is still with the Lame, the victim. Andy and I were uncertain about all the finer aspects of the Pocketbook Drop, also known as the Pigeon Drop but realized that Detective George's assumption had to be true, if not these females would have left this area immediately. Drag girls do not remain in the area if the victim does not accept their story, they quickly take off. The fact that these girls behaved like a Drag team indicated to us that they had to have another partner who is still with the Lame. After about 10 minutes the Mish was prepared and the Drag girl who had arrived late, left the car. I followed on foot, while Detective George and Andy remained with the driver of the car, since that would be the final means of leaving the area for all the Drag girls once the score was made.

The driver started the car and proceeded to pull the car up the block to a different spot closer to a Jug, the bank on the corner. Meanwhile I observed the Drag girl enter a nearby restaurant and join two other females who were in conversation. I saw one of the Drag girls leave the table and enter the lady's room. What appeared as a normal action was later to be realized the place where the Lame's money was switched from one envelope to another. The Lame received one envelope containing play money rather than an envelope with her own money. The Lame had withdrawn $1,500 from the Jug (bank), to show the Drag girl good faith, thus sharing in the found money of $33,000. The switch had been so smooth in this case that later we were to learn the switch requires dexterity to avoid having the Lame realize what is happening. Most switches occur in the presence of the Lame, in cars, on street corners, or in houses. However, in this case the Lame was so conned, the hit girl, the one who found the money, took the Lame's money from her, and made the switch in the seclusion of the lady's bathroom.

The Lame and the two Drag girls left the restaurant and walked to a nearby office building. I observed one of the Drag girls pointing the Lame to this building. In this stage, the Lame left the two Drag girls and walked toward that building. I realized that the switch of the envelopes had obviously been made and the Drag girls were leaving the area. They started to run in the direction of the car operated by the third partner. I gave a thumbs up to signal Andy and Detective George that the ruse had been completed. The two Drag girls jumped into the car and were about to pull away when Detective George and Andy pulled in front of their car and jumped out, surrounding the car, and reached in grabbing their pocketbooks to recover the evidence. As they did this the Drag girls began to scream. It was later realized that this outburst was a ploy used when arrested. It gave the impression to curious onlookers that muggers were attempting to grab their pocketbooks. It was hoped that in the confusion the Drag girls could escape. Detective George quickly yelled to Andy and me, "Get the cuffs, get the cuffs." In our haste we left our handcuffs back in his vehicle. We yelled at George, "Where are your cuffs?" his face turned a bright red as he muttered in a subdued way, "They are in my car's glove box." A retired detective working in a nearby building saw the commotion. Detective George recognized the retired detective and asked him for his cuffs. This individual ran back into the building to retrieve his handcuffs from his desk without asking or saying anything, quite embarrassing for all. Our vehicle was nearby, I retrieved all the cuffs while Andy and Detective George held the Drag girls as well as controlling the crowd that started to gather.

A senior citizen who was watching the action on the street remarked to the crowd, "Those men should be ashamed of themselves, grabbing those pocketbooks that way. I thought purse snatchers were much younger, what is this world coming too?" We quickly shuffled the Drag girls into Detective

George's vehicle making our way to the precinct. By this time, a marked police unit came by and took two of the three Drag girls in their unit back to the precinct.

Once at the precinct a search of the girls recovered an envelope containing the $1,500 in cash. Only one problem now remained, who and where was the Lame. She was still walking around the area with the switched envelope looking for the so-called lawyer to show her good faith money to him. I hurried back to the scene to find her, eventually locating her in the lobby of the office building she had been sent to by the Drag girls. After showing her my ID and badge, I attempted to explain the story to her of what had happened. I told her, you were approached by two girls who stated they had found an envelope containing a sum of money. The Lame did not respond. I realizing the Lame is not about to admit that she was willing to share in the found money without reporting it to the police, as I patiently continued to relate the story. I told the Lame that I knew she is in possession of an envelope she thinks contains her money she is planning to take to the lawyer as directed by the Drag girls.

I continued the story by saying, "The envelope you have does not contain your money, nor is there any lawyer to see in this building. We have your money at the police precinct as well as the girls to whom you were talking." When the Lame refused to acknowledge that she understood what I was talking about, I tried a different approach. I said, "If there is any money in that envelope you have, I will double whatever amount is in there." I walked outside, knowing I had made my point. The Lame's hurried steps in my direction, revealing to me that she must have opened the envelope. She ran up to me screaming, "My money, my money, where is it?" I took her to the precinct for the necessary identification of the females involved.

At the precinct, I brought the Lame into the Burglary Squad office. She was quite shaken up by the ordeal, so we sent out for coffee. She proceeded to spill it all over the pants of one of the precinct detectives in the room with us. She properly identified the two females we had seen running from the scene with her money. Both Andy and I were happy knowing we saved someone's money today and arrested three individuals in the process. Detective George appeared relaxed for the first time in over a week, but he was extremely cautious about safeguarding the switched money. Andy and I joked to ourselves that he was concerned we might try to switch envelopes with him. We had a good laugh.

The Lame kept insisting that she needed all her money back right away and was a little put out that it was needed as evidence. She complained that her husband would find out she withdrew it without his knowledge and that would not be good for her relationship. The Lame still had not taken the time to thank us for recovering her money, she continued to complain about the delay and her husband's vicious temper. In the subsequent court appearance in this case, we had to pick up the Lame at various locations other than her residence.

She still had not told her husband about this episode and was not going to. She was constantly in fear of his finding out about the case; therefore, we were compelled to honor her cloak and dagger style meetings. We were glad that we had vouchered her money as evidence rather than return it to her in the beginning. We felt this was the only thing that kept her coming to court for this case. On one occasion I called her to remind her of a court appearance date. However, a man's voice was heard on the phone. Remembering that she did not have any person living with her in her home but her husband, I pulled my own ruse to cover the call. I stated I was a salesperson for Time Magazine, a gimmick I used to pull off successfully in past cases to secure information. I was calling to offer a special package for a one-year subscription. I was so convincing that the husband agreed to purchase the one-year subscription exclusive offer. I had a chuckle in later years recalling this event, and often wondered if the husband ever checked back with the magazine when he did not receive the billing or the order.

Six additional arrests on other schemes followed in rapid order during the following three weeks. Detective George informed us that he was returning to his unit and that we were on our own. He stated whether our temporary assignment extended beyond the summer, which would depend on how well we succeeded. George did not give any hints whether he approved or disapproved our performance while we were with him. Nor did he indicate what he thought our chances were of continuing this assignment. That was his style.

However, we thought inwardly he approved of our work and felt we would make it beyond the summer peak season. It was only much later when we started to excel more in this field that we received undertones from those that knew Detective George. It seems whenever we made a good collar, arrest in subsequent months, George would comment to whomever he was with saying, "I turned them out." When word would filter back to Andy and me about George's comments, we considered it a strong endorsement, even though he was patting himself on the back.

After Detective George's departure we were on our own and finally we got our own vehicle, a 1969 Mercury that had been confiscated in a narcotics bust. It was not the best, we thought, but it was wheels. However, the most important thing it had was a working air conditioner and that it represented a sign of recognition that we made the summit at this early stage. Each month that went by remaining on this detail became more important to us. We were productive and it felt like somebody recognized our performance.

CHAPTER 1

INTELLIGENCE GATHERING AND THE BIRTH OF BACKSTAGE & SOFT-SHOES

The New York City Police Department was sued, we were forced to return the 1969 Mercury back to the owner. This left Andy and I once again without a vehicle. The Commanding Officer of the Queens Burglary Squad made phone calls and was able to get another vehicle for us to use. Unfortunately, this was a yellow Checker Taxicab. This was not a good vehicle to use following anyone in certain areas of Queens, where a yellow taxi would never drive through.

If a victim reported a fraud where there was a loss, we would schedule our tour the next day to come in during the evening so we could conduct the investigation and interview the victim. After the interview, Andy and I would review the recent arrests of individuals fitting the description given by the Lame. If the Lame identified one or more individuals as the people responsible for the fraud, Andy or I would fill out a Police Department Wanted Card, which identified those individuals. This card would remain on file in the event they were arrested again. Andy or I would be notified if arrested and we would try to get to court within the authority of New York City to re-arrest the individuals before they got out on bail. On occasions, Andy and I were notified late, and the subject(s) left court and never returned to court. A warrant for their arrest was issued by the court.

Before going out on patrol/surveillance, Andy and I would review all the larceny cases that were reported in our Detective District. From this information we were able to target certain areas based on those cases reported. A great deal of the reported frauds were in areas where a yellow taxi would never be seen. This created a real problem for Andy and me. To try to overcome this disadvantage, we used disguises and props such as wigs and a suitcase. I would sit in the rear of the taxicab as a passenger and exit the cab carrying the suitcase.

On one occasion working in the 103rd Precinct near the Jamaica Bus Terminal on 168th Street we noticed two males engaged in conversation with a female Lame. It looked like we had a Stuff game in progress. We kept them under observation, and I exited the cab and approached the group carrying a suitcase. As I got closer, I saw the handkerchief in the hand of one of the men. At that point, the man became nervous and started to run. By this time Andy had exited the taxicab and was on foot. He gave chase to the second man who also started to run leaving the female Lame standing there. I grabbed the one con artist with the Stuff in his hand, the Handkerchief. I dragged him toward a parked car and handcuffed him to the car door handle. At that point, I realized he was missing one leg. The con artist had a false leg, and it came off while he was dragged to the car to be handcuffed. His leg was in the middle of the street. I immediately went over to the Lame and explained what was happening. She thanked me for saving her the money, which would not have happened if we did not interfere. Andy arrested the second subject. Both subjects appeared in court the following day for arraignment. At the arraignment, the player with the one leg came into court on crutches. The judge presiding over his bail hearing was upset that we arrested a one-legged man. I had the opportunity to explain to the judge that he had a false leg at the time of the crime, and I did not know this until he was arrested. Both were held with no bail.

A week passed using this yellow taxicab. Andy and I reached out to the NYPD Motor Pool and asked if they could paint our cab black. We would then be using it as a gypsy cab. These are unlicensed vehicles like the one assigned to Andy and me. The gypsy cabs worked in areas where no yellow licensed cab would enter and offer services to locals. It took two days to paint the taxicab. Andy and I were back in business.

It was a beautiful Wednesday, and the temperature was about 75 degrees, and people were out walking on the street. We decided to use the new black taxicab on this day. We had administrative work to do first before leaving the office. It was around 2pm before we were able to leave the desk work. This is late in the day and most frauds (scores) have already occurred. We decided to ride the parkway and observe vehicles heading back into Manhattan. I was wearing a blonde wig and seated in the front seat of the cab next to Andy. Jokingly, I placed my hand on Andy's leg and he jumped, causing the car to accelerate and strike the vehicle in front of us. It was an embarrassing situation when a marked uniform patrol car came by to do the accident report. Of course, at that point, I had removed the wig. So much for disguises.

Intelligence Gathering

In most arrests Andy and I made, the individuals had street names. Examples were Bo, Tilly, and Cool Breeze. When questioned, the arrested would tell us they know their partners involved in the fraud only by their street name. Looking at the address books found on the arrested, they had names as well as street names and phone numbers. We decided to take this information from everyone we arrested and enter the data on index cards as intelligence for future reference. We created an index file by phone number, the subject's name, date when arrested, and the street name of each person listed in that telephone book. Every card was referenced back to the individual who was arrested and had this information in their possession. The cards were filed numerically by phone number and alphabetically by name. For example, if we identified a person for a previous fraud and we knew his street name, we could go to this file and find phone number/s for that individual. We checked the numbers with the telephone company who gave us an address of where to find that individual. This file was helpful in solving past confidence games, thus clearing open cases. This filing system took time to create using a typewriter. So many of those arrested by Andy and I had a full telephone book in their possession. Every day at the start of our tour, I would work on the index card file and Andy would review the reported crimes the day before in Queens to see if there were any frauds to be investigated. This was around 1973 long before computers came into the picture.

The Birth of Backstage and Soft-Shoes
During our first 11 months together, Andy and I made over eighty arrests. Our success in the 16th Detective District came to the attention of the Queens borough commander.

The commander asked us to join him and our lieutenant at a meeting. At the meeting, the borough commander wanted the Confidence Team to expand its role from one detective district to the entire borough of Queens. This would entail all reported confidence game cases be assigned to the newly named, Queens Confidence Team (Andy and I). All confidence game investigations would be referred to us, which would give us a greater area to patrol and surveil.

One day after taking two female prisoners to our office to be booked, one of the females mentioned Andy's shoes and called them Soft-Shoes. At the same time this prisoner mentioned that she never saw me prior to the arrest and stated I was hidden or backstage. The next day we decided to take street names, Backstage and Soft-Shoes and let our prisoners know who had arrested them using our new street names going forward. After 11 months of this assignment, we realized that we needed to send a strong message that confidence games were not permitted in the borough of Queens. We could achieve this by letting every confidence operator we came across know that there are two Bunco Rollers by the name Backstage and Soft-Shoes working in Queens. Bunco Rollers is the street name used by confidence operators for the police who know confidence games. We felt we could psychologically put fear into these individuals and stop them from coming to Queens. This was our assignment to stop or reduce this type of larceny. In addition, we instituted a business card informing the individual, "You are under arrest for the Drag or the Stuff - Backstage and Soft-Shoes." Each card had number, 1-10 printed across the top. The prisoners were told to present this card the next time they were arrested and to ask the arresting officer to punch one number. When you reached ten, you received a free get-out-of-jail opportunity. This was done as a joke to break the ice when we arrested someone and to help spread our reputation.

I received a call one day from a detective in the Baltimore Maryland Police Department who was also a Bunco Roller. He asked me about the business card. He had made an arrest of a team, and they presented their cards to him to be punched. Upon hearing this both Andy and I started laughing, this joke was working. The detective did what we asked and punched their card. We explained to the detective, this was another way of spreading our reputation. This idea of using street names took a little time to reach the confidence community, which operated primarily out of the borough of Manhattan. Every arrest we made going forward, we would identify ourselves as Backstage and Soft-Shoes. After a while, our real names, Ted Farace and Andy Camera were unknown names, only being recognized by our street names. This idea was also working. We started to see a reduction of reported cases of completed confidence games, especially the (Drag) or Pocketbook Drop or Pigeon Drop, the Handkerchief Switch, (the Stuff), which made the borough commander incredibly happy. We still were able to affect street arrests on attempted confidence games based on observations, but not affecting the number of arrests that we made during our first 11 months.

With the slowdown of reported cases, we, the Queens Confidence Team, began to focus on other types of swindles, such as the Phony VCR/TV fraud and Gypsies committing fraud using their con game, the Bajour Blessing. The Gypsies would claim there was a curse on the individual's money, stating they can help remove it. Also, the Gypsies were at the time invading homes of the elderly in Queens burglarizing their homes. In addition, home repair con men called The Scottish Tinkers who were also called the Williamson family. These individuals would travel across the country especially in the spring and summer, offering home repairs to elderly unsuspected victims. The repairs never took place such as fixing the roof and then collecting payment from the homeowner without any repair being made. These home repair individuals would travel from State to State and had no real roots. The Confidence Team also worked on "Slummers." These were individuals who would offer gold chains or expensive watches at a discount price on the street to unsuspecting victims, when in fact they were knockoffs of real products and worthless.

In early spring and up to the fall in New York City, this was a prime time for South American pickpockets and Spanish confidence game operators. The nice weather in New York at that time made it easier for pickpockets to steal from victims wearing less clothing. In South America it was winter, so the pickpockets and con men and women would fly up to New York City and work there for months, then travel to other major cities, flying back home to South America. The Spanish con operators came mostly from Columbia. In Queens there was a large population of Spanish speaking families living in Jackson Heights, Corona, and Flushing, which made this area ripe for the Spanish con game. Pickpockets worked mostly in New York City with large crowds on the streets and in big retail stores. The Spanish con game worked like the Pocketbook Drop or Drag. It was done by two, three, or four individuals, both male and female, all speaking Spanish. These type of confidence games were very rarely reported to the police. Many of the victims would not call the police because of embarrassment after being fleeced.

CHAPTER 2

WHAT ARE CONFIDENCE GAMES

Authoring this book, it was necessary to explain the various confidence games we will be focusing on over the next few chapters.

The "Drag" Known As The Pocketbook Drop
Or Pigeon Drop

The victim who is approached on the street or inside a store by one con artist and shows the victim an envelope or bag containing a hefty sum of money. A Michigan bank role or the street term a Mish, which she states was found on the street. A second con artist joins the conversation and offers to help. The first con artist has a knowledgeable and trustworthy friend, such as an attorney and she will seek his advice. The second con artist and the Lame remain together, either on the street or in a nearby restaurant while the first con artist goes to a nearby office building to talk with the attorney. The first con artist returns and convinces the Lame and the second con artist to go to their banks and withdraw a sum of money as a sign of good faith. That money is placed in other envelopes and taken to the attorney by the first con artist. This is to ensure the attorney has proof that each party can live on their own money for at least 90 days in the event someone comes forward claiming they lost the money without using their share of the found money. Upon return, the first con artist gives back an envelope to each, the Lame and the second con artist allegedly containing the good faith money and their share of the found money. These envelopes contained paper only. Both subjects walk away leaving the Lame swindled. There are variations in this swindle, but it is all about found money.

The 'Stuff' Known as the Handkerchief Switch
Or Jamaica Handkerchief Switch

This fraud has variations as well. The difference is the fake roll of money Mish or Michigan bank roll, is rolled up in a handkerchief and switched by one of the confidence men. Males primarily play this swindle. One approaches an individual Lame on the street and asks for help. He is from Jamaica and speaks little English. He shows the Lame a small slip of paper, written on it is the word Brownstone apartment with an address and a note that says paid $100.00. The street address is bogus and does not exist. This individual who is new to this country tells the Lame that it was just dropped off by a cab driver and he is looking for the address. At this point, a second male after overhearing part of the conversation joins the two and offers to help. The Jamaican pulls out a roll of money, the Mish, and shows it to the Lame and second con artist. He is told it is not safe to do that and urges the Jamaican to place his money in a bank for safekeeping. The Jamaican tells them he does not trust banks. The Jamaican tells the Lame and the second con artist that he wants them to hold his money until he can find a place to live. He asks both the Lame and the second one who joined the conversation to place their money into a handkerchief as a sign of good faith and asks the Lame to hold all the money. The Lame must go to the bank and withdraw money, while the second con artist has cash on him, which he showed the Lame. Both then place their money into the handkerchief with the Mish, a roll of fake money, and the Lame is distracted by one of the con artists as the handkerchief is switched and given to the Lame for safekeeping. All three leave with the Lame holding what he or she believe to be the money, when in fact it contains only cut up paper.

Phony TV-VCR Swindle

The swindle could involve any product in demand at the time, including at one time Anti-Freeze. This type of swindle is committed by individuals that are opportunists. They see a product that is expensive and use that product to dupe victims into believing they are getting a good deal on that product, such as color TV's or VCR's. The con operators would make phone calls to potential victims until they have someone interested in this swindle; offering a product for sale at a discounted rate or sometimes they allude that the goods are stolen property. They state the item, a TV or VCR is overstocked, and the store needs to reduce inventory. After convincing a victim at that point, the victim is instructed to meet the contact for this deal at a major department store and pick up the merchandise. The victim is told to bring a pickup truck to load the goods. Once at the location, the victim is approached by the con operator and picks up the money for the goods. The victim is told to back their truck into the loading bay of the store and wait for the goods to be brought out from the store. The con operator leaves the victim and enters the loading bay door leading into the store. He leaves by the front door, leaving the victim still waiting for the so-called goods in the loading bay area.

Gypsy Blessing Swindles
Gypsies participate in these types of swindles, from auto repairs on the street to Tarot Card readings and blessing swindles. They also participate in burglaries of homes of the elderly. Recently, they have been known to be Slummers selling gold bracelets or chains and watches that are knock offs and worthless to unsuspecting victims. The most profitable for the Gypsies is the Bajour or Blessing Swindle. A victim comes for a Tarot card reading and the female Gypsy realizes they can now offer the blessing to this victim claiming the victim's money is the curse on that person and they can remove it. The victim could have love issues or health issues, and that person is told the root cause is her money. The victim is told to bring cash so it can be ceremoniously destroyed, thus lifting the curse on the victim. During this ceremony, the Gypsy will crack open an egg, which is filled with red dye

telling the victim this is not a good sign. The victim is asked to place a sum of money into a handkerchief, which will be burned to lift the curse. During the conversation, the victim is distracted, and the handkerchief is switched to one containing cut up paper and that one is destroyed. This Bajour could go on for months after the initial swindle with more money being allegedly destroyed.

It is important to note that the female Gypsies are the most valuable in the family. They do all the swindles while the males do the low-end swindle, such as body work in the street and selling knock off goods. There is no education within the Gypsy families, all are self-taught at home with no schooling. Gypsies are also known to use a ruse of a pregnant women seeking a glass of water by knocking on the door of an elderly homeowner. Once inside the residence a second subject, a male accomplice enters the home and walks around unnoticed by the resident who is occupied helping the alleged pregnant female. This second individual ransacks the home looking for valuables to steal. Gypsies also ride around in the spring and summer months seeking older people offering to coat their driveways. This is only a color, which washes off as soon as it gets wet.

Slummers
This swindle is less known than the ones described above. Individuals would purchase knockoffs of gold chains, bracelets, and watches. They would approach individuals on the street, in a store or casino and offer those items for

sale. The victim thinks they are getting a good deal when in fact they are worthless.

Williamson's Family Or Scottish Tinkers Scam

This swindle involves individuals passing themselves to the victim as contractors able to fix or repair a roof or a driveway. These individuals come from Scottish backgrounds and usually travel from other states. They have pickup trucks with out-of-state license plates. The pickups have ladders and other tools in the back to appear as a contractor. This type of swindle occurs in the warmer months, May to September, in the New York City area. The con artist travels in residential areas seeking seniors outdoors working on their lawn. They tell the senior the roof needs repair and if not fixed, it could collapse. The senior hires them to fix the issue. They place their ladders against the house for a period appearing to be up on the roof fixing the problem. They approach the homeowner for payment, and on occasion while the homeowner is inside the house getting the payment, the swindlers may wander inside the house stealing whatever item of value, they can find.

CHAPTER 3

THE INFORMANT

The Initial Encounter

One day in the spring of 1975, after spending much of the day catching up on our administrative work, Andy and I decided that, even though it was late in the day, we would go out on surveillance. We were not sure what we would find because the banks were already closed which meant that if a confidence game were to occur, it would have already happened.

We decided to watch the highway coming from Nassau and Suffolk Counties heading toward Manhattan for any suspicious vehicles. We were looking for any teams that might be heading back to the city. As we were driving toward the entrance to the parkway leading to Manhattan, we observed a vehicle with out of state license plates occupied by two females about to enter the highway. We put that vehicle under surveillance.

The vehicle did not enter the parkway but proceeded to turn onto a street that was part of a small middle-class neighborhood near the entrance to the parkway. We followed it for a period and when the vehicle "squared the block," it told us they had recognized us as police. The suspect's car proceeded to enter the parkway heading back into the city. At this point, we decided to pull the vehicle over close to the Triborough Bridge entrance for a spot check.

Once the vehicle stopped, I exited our car and walked over to the driver's side of the car. I identified myself as a police officer and showed the driver my detective badge. The female driver was asked to produce her license and registration. She complied, handing me a State of Florida driver's license. I looked at it and knew it was a bogus license. I chuckled at the license to let her know I knew it was fake and then said, "I bet my partner you have a "pack" in your purse." She pretended to look a little confused but with a great big smile said, "a pack of cigarettes?" I said no. Never asking why they were stopped or what this was all about, she opened her purse for me to inspect. Finding nothing, she asked if I wanted to do the same with her partner. I said no. She even offered to open her trunk, but by their willingness to comply I knew they had disposed of it somehow. Later that day I found out that when they "squared the block" the driver stopped short at a trash bin and the woman in the passenger seat jumped out and disposed of all the paraphernalia (pack). I proceeded to get their registration which listed a male with an out of state address as the owner of the car. Upon returning to the office, I determined the address was that of an empty lot. This is a common practice that confidence operators use to registering their cars with an out of state phony address.

I inquired where they were coming from. The driver indicated they were visiting friends in Nassau County. Andy and I did not believe this story; confidence operators lie about everything. I looked at the driver and told her that I did not believe the name on the license was her real name and then said "I may not know your real name yet, but I know what you are up to…you two are hustlers, confidence players, playing the Drag. Do you know how I know that? Because we are Bunco Rollers and my name is Backstage, and my partner's name is Soft-Shoes, you've heard of us." The driver did not answer or say anything, but by the look on her face, it was evident that what I had just said was true. I handed the license back to the driver and said "Mary Rodgers from Boca Raton, Florida, which is not you, this is your lucky day! We are not going to take you and your partner in for investigation, but I promise you this, we will see you again." Then, before letting them go, I gave the occupants a final warning that if they came through Queens again, they would be arrested immediately. They drove off into Manhattan. It was only a matter of time that our paths would cross again.

"I Knew I'd See You Again!"
A year or so later, I received a call from a detective regarding a prisoner they had arrested and was being held in the Nassau County Jail. He said this female prisoner wanted

to cooperate and asked to speak with Backstage. As it turned out, the Nassau County detective knew our street names and about the work we were doing as the Queens Confidence Team.

I drove to the Nassau County Jail the following day while Andy remained in the office handling other issues. I met the detective who informed me they had a female under arrest for a felony con game. A police officer had apprehended her coming out of Bonwit Teller, a department store, located in the Miracle Mile in Manhasset, Long Island. According to the report, two females were in the store attempting to speak with one of the store's patrons. Something did not feel quite right to the store detective, so he called the police. When they saw the police coming, her partner, who must have been the driver, jumped into their car to escape. When she tried to get in the moving car her partner locked the doors and proceeded to begin to exit the parking lot. She tried to jump on the hood of the car, but it was too late, the police officer grabbed her, and she was arrested.

When the detective ran a check on the name she was using, she was identified as a wanted felon. Once she was fingerprinted, the out-of-state governor's warrants were filed against her; two of which were from Broward County, Florida and a third from Atlanta, Georgia. This required her to be held without bail until her case in Nassau came up on the court calendar and a disposition was obtained. She would then be extradited to those states to face those charges.

As soon as I walked into the interview room, I recognized her as the female driver we had let go by the Triborough Bridge. "See, I told you I'd see you again!" Mary Rodgers, which was the alias she had given me a year ago, nodded but there was no big smile this time. The meeting started off cordially enough and after minutes of conversation, I asked her what she wanted to talk about. She began by explaining she had been running con games for quite a while and was really worried now that she would be going to jail for years because of those out-of-state warrants. She now had a daughter and desperately did not want her little girl to grow up without a mother. After talking with her for a while that day I found out that she played the Pigeon Drop or Drag across the country. She had been in numerous states committing these frauds for some time and had a wealth of intelligence information that law enforcement could use. For me, this was a good opportunity to gain more knowledge and a greater understanding of how things worked from the inside.

For her, becoming a mother had changed everything and she wanted out of that life. She admitted to me she was on heroin and wanted to get into a program to clean herself up. She wanted to be drug free and raise her child under better conditions. Eventually she did get into a 9-month live-in program that took mothers and their babies. She got "straight" and never looked back. I took a chance on someone that day and I am proud to say it worked. As a police officer most of your time is spent catching and convicting criminals. That was the usually the end story, and if you ever did see them again on the street, unfortunately, it was most probably to arrest them on an added charge. So, being able to go beyond the conviction and see it through to a successful new beginning for someone was very gratifying.

At the time of the arrest, Judith (the name we will use for our Informant) was living with a man, ten years her senior, who was well connected in the confidence world. He came from a family of hustlers. He had grown up around his father, brother and uncle who were all players. He told her that he had never held a legitimate job. He learned how to con people out of their money as a teenager from his family. He was a "slickster." Judith said that although she might have been blinded by having money again and having fun buying new clothes and jewelry, in the beginning, she didn't feel like that anymore. It was all wrong and she knew it. Plus, he was the one calling all the shots while she was the one running the risk of going to jail. She wanted out of the game and away from their relationship which had become very abusive over time.

Our conversation continued for over an hour or so. In that conversation she agreed to assist the Queens Confidence Team by supplying information on other wanted confidence criminals. The deal was to help us and in exchange we would do our best to help her with those out-of-state court cases. This was a big hurdle to overcome for me, considering I would have to convince three jurisdictions including Nassau County to withdraw their warrants and release her from jail to assist us on outstanding investigations. Judith was told that I would have to register her as a New York City Police Informant. She had no problem with this. She would cooperate in any way she could to get help. She also had spoken to the man she was living with to make sure he was on board with this, which he was. In truth he was key because he had so much more information than she did. He had the connections across the country. Judith said there were players all over the country and they all knew each other. Plus, he wanted Judith out of jail asap. She understood that future meetings would take place on a regular basis, after I had, hopefully, obtained approval and completed all the paperwork necessary to register her as an Informant. The Nassau County detective who contacted me was not opposed to her helping us if there were results that could benefit his agency as well. I asked him to research his files in Nassau County for any wanted individuals that we might be able to find and prosecute with Judith's help. The detective was not entirely convinced that she would keep her word to work as an Informant once released back into the streets. He felt she might be conning me being that she was a "sweet talker." Time would tell if this was true or not.

Judith's case was on the court calendar three weeks away, which did not give me a great deal of time to achieve her release. The first hurdle to overcome was gaining approval from the lieutenant in the Burglary Squad. He had to run it by the borough commander. When it was finally approved, I had to register Judith and obtain a NYPD registered Informant serial number. After a good deal of paperwork, her registration was processed and approved. A follow up meeting was held with Judith in the Nassau County Jail where I informed her that the registration was approved and that now I needed to get her released to work for us as our confidential Informant.

I set up a meeting with the then district attorney, John Santucci's office to get his office on board with releasing Judith to assist us with outstanding Queens warrants and investigations. Affecting arrests pertaining to any Queens outstanding warrants would benefit the Queens District Attorney. Once we had his blessing, the next step was for the Nassau County District Attorney's Office to agree to release her to my custody and to hold off their prosecution, pending results of her help. After achieving this, I needed to get an agreement from Georgia and Florida to withdraw their warrants so I could get her out of jail. Over the next few weeks, I was in contact with the Georgia authorities on the felony warrant that was placed on her. After a discussion, the Prosecutors office in Georgia agreed to place their case on hold and release her with the understanding that she had to appear in court one year later to answer the charge. When I met with Judith to let her know that Georgia had agreed to her release, she was relieved and grateful.

The last step was convincing the Broward County Sheriff's office to agree to the release and withdraw the two holds on Judith. The detective on both investigations in Florida was adamant about not releasing her. He was against this and agreed with the Nassau County detective that she was conning me. To gain his confidence, I called him and made an offer, like a bet, of my paycheck against his check that Judith would surrender to him in Florida one year from the date of her release. The detective took the bait and agreed to work with us. He went to the prosecutor, and they also withdrew their arrests warrants. Another meeting was held with Judith in the Nassau County Jail, and she was informed that all the holds on her were lifted, and she was free to go. I gave her stipulations, one being, only one year on the street and then back to court in Georgia, Florida, and Nassau County to face those pending charges. She agreed to the one year "stay" and understood she needed to check-in with me at least once a week and that if she did not the whole thing was off! I then reviewed all necessary information from her, including her most current address, phone number, the make, model, and license plate number of the car she would be driving plus complete information on who she was living with. Then came the moment she had been waiting for, released on her own recognizance, Judith walked out of the Nassau County jail.

Life started up again like nothing had ever happened, but everything was different. She kept current with her phone calls and began gathering information on the various names we were giving her. She continued in her relationship so as not to raise any red flags but this time she had a real exit plan.

Over the next couple of months everything went as planned. Our weekly phone conversations, which sometimes lasted a couple of hours, gave me the opportunity to gain information about the confidence field nationwide. I would mention a street name and ask Judith to find out if this person was in town and where he was staying. Since Judith's relationship still appeared to be in decent shape, she had no problem obtaining the information. All this valuable information was added to The Queens Confidence Intelligence files to be used in future investigations. Andy and I affected arrests based on information we obtained from our Informant of individuals having outstanding warrants in Queens, New York prior to the formation of the Confidence Team. The Queens District Attorney's office was pleased with our progress. We were beginning to see results of the agreement we had with Judith.

Her Story

Every week when she checked in, over the one-year period that she was out of jail, I had the opportunity to speak at length about her life. It was a natural progression in this situation. Aside from the "official" business of information gathering I could not help but be curious as to how a well brought up girl could wind up a heroin addict playing con games. Judith said it started over a fight concerning her mother's sweater. She told me that when she ran away, she had only lived with her mother and stepfather for fourteen months. Prior to that she had been raised initially by grandparents and then sent to boarding schools.

One night in April of 1968, Judith had a fight with her mother. She had borrowed a sweater without permission. They wound up in a yelling match and she told her mother that she hated it there or something like that. The next morning when Judith called her mother's office to make up and told me her mother was extremely cold and said, "Oh you mean you're staying?" and she said, "Oh you mean I can go?" "Yes" she said, "if you can find a friend's family who will take you in, yes you can go." Judith said she hung up the phone and just sat there stunned. Judith did not know "how" to leave but she told me she knew she could not stay. Judith left home that day with absolutely nothing and became a "runaway."

As it turned out, she did not have to run far. She called a friend who went to school with her and lived in the same building on the East Side of Manhattan. He called friends and found a place on the West Side where she could stay temporarily. Judith said she got lucky because the brownstone where she wound up was filled with mostly young and interesting people. The apartment doors were left open so you could poke your head in to say hi. Hippies and drugs were everywhere. Summer evenings were spent staying up all night in Washington Square on meth (also called speed) talking about politics and philosophy, dropping LSD (acid), and fiercely debating whether God existed. She was always on God's side. Many of her friends had started snorting heroin. It was the one drug she had not tried but eventually caved because it was so cheap, and everyone was raving about it. $2.00 for a bag was all you needed!

The first time she tried it, she told me she threw up and thought it was awful. The second time she wound up riding a bus in New York City, way past her stop because she kept falling asleep, but not really, she was "nodding." What she did notice about this drug, was it got rid of a feeling deep within her that had hurt and haunted her since she was a child. Nothing had ever made that go away. Her childhood psychiatrist described it as her "black hole" or pit.

Living the hippie life went on for a couple of years until someone asked her if she had ever done a speedball. She relayed to me that she had never done it. This man was a drug dealer (and user) and told her she would get a better high if she shot it, plus she would be shooting cocaine along with the heroin. Judith told me she had never used needles, but he was convincing (not that she needed much at that point) and she replied, "OK." He "cooked" her speedball in a spoon and slowly injected it into her. She had never felt anything like that and related to me that she could still remember hearing Steve Wonder sing "For Once in My Life" in the background and how incredible she felt. It was all downhill from there. Her group of friends, who were getting pretty messed up as well, dwindled down to people who were going to shoot up. She described for me what a "shooting gallery" or "get-off house" was like, and it wasn't pretty. It was a group of people with needles hanging out of their arms, their heads nodding, saying little in a dimly lit room that stunk of stale cigarettes and body odor. It was the summertime, and she was experiencing a genuine issue with money or rather the lack of. The problem was her $2.00 bag was now $10.00, and she was becoming a real junkie by now with a habit that had to be fed several times a day. She was so lonely, felt so unloved and so messed up that the "get-off" rooms became her home.

Occasionally she would chat with one guy who dressed exceptionally well for someone shooting dope in a "get-off house." One day she asked him what he did for a living since his clothes looked so expensive. He told her that if she were interested, he could show her a way to make money, a great deal of money. She knew that girls who were using drugs prostituted to make money, and she did not want to do that. He assured her that this money had nothing to do with selling her body. He said he was a hustler not a pimp. She became interested, at least enough to hear him out, so she decided to get lunch and talk.

The man said he had once been in the exact same position she was in, a dope fiend who did not have money. She told me she was totally interested but she didn't want to have to stick somebody up with a gun or hurt anybody. When she mentioned that to him, he told her that he did not do that kind of stuff, words were his only weapon. She had no idea what he was talking about, but it sounded like a fantastic way to make money. Again, he explained to her that he was a hustler who played con games namely the Pigeon Drop or Drag, the Stuff and the Comeback scam. He suggested to Judith that she should learn the Pigeon Drop because men mostly played the Comeback swindle and the Stuff. She asked him, was this Pigeon Drop hard to learn? Did he think she could even do it, and more importantly would she be any good at it? Judith was told that she was perfect for it. Not only did she look the part, but she had the gift of gab and that was key! He asked Judith to meet him the next day in the Bronx, and he would introduce her to a couple of players.

One of those players she was to meet was a man that she heard was a bad ass in this field. He was one of the best and most respected players. Judith was excited. The next day she met them in the Bronx at a luncheonette. They had coffee and then she was invited over to their apartment. (They wanted to check her out first before inviting her over). Judith explained she was nervous when she got there because she had no idea what she was doing. They told her to relax and just tell them a little bit about herself. Figuring she should get it out of the way first, Judith told them she used drugs, specifically heroin mostly and sometimes heroin and coke. He told her, if it did not affect the way she presented herself or how she played the game, it was cool.

Classroom Training

Judith went on to describe how these men had a great deal of energy, but she could tell they were serious about this game. They were all business that first day. She described the apartment to me; she sat in a chair in the living room, while the others sat across from her. Judith mentioned there was also a woman who lived there who said hello and was cordial but clearly gave off the feeling she was not thrilled about Judith being in her home. (Just a note: Judith said she was the only white person in the apartment). During the conversation one male called out, "Catch," he tossed her what looked like money all rolled up with a rubber band around it. There was a $100 bill on top. She had no idea what this was. She was told it is called a Michigan Bankroll. Judith was asked to take the rubber band off look at the other bills.

Judith did that. There were two $100 bills in this "Michigan Bankroll" and sandwiched in between them was a big stack of one-dollar bills. It was impressive looking and if you did not pull the whole thing apart it would look like a lot of money which, of course, was the whole point! She was instructed to use real bills, not play money. One of the males picked up a manila envelope and put the money in it. It was explained to her that this envelope with cash inside was called a "pack" and was told if your partner asks if you have the "pack" you know what it means.

Judith was asked to pretend you are out on the street and you just saw this envelope on the ground. She was instructed to pick it up and start to open it. Once you realize there is money in there close it back up and look shocked, a little scared and confused. Judith was told that she will be doing this for the benefit of the Mark and that you and your partner have chosen so you want to make sure she sees you pick it up. Then act as if you are clearly upset when the Mark asks if you're okay. She was told to slightly open the envelope and pull the money up enough for the Mark to get a glimpse of it and see that there's A LOT of money in there. Just flash it she was told. This was important to pull off the con. Put the envelope into your purse right away. At this point Judith should pull her partner in, or maybe not. Only after Judith was sure this person was buying the story, should she call for her partner to come in. It's important that you want to make sure of a couple of things, is the victim wise to the game and if she says she is, ask her to explain. Sometimes they may have heard a warning about con games but that's it. Judith needed to find out what the Mark knew because later when she takes the Mark to her bank she would need to prep her about what the bank teller or manager might ask. For example, they might ask her if she knows what a con game is. Judith should give them an answer to that question and was told to make the Mark practice it out loud. A suggestion would be, "This withdrawal is going to be a wonderful surprise wedding gift for my son and although it's a bit wild, cash is so much more exciting than a check. Now how much longer will I have to wait for my withdrawal? I've got a lot to do today!" Judith was also told that she should find out if there is anything the victim must do that day or anyone she must meet that could get in the way of this "sting" happening.

She was instructed on when it's time to bring your partner in, you signal them by pulling on your collar or your sleeve. This says, "all is good, let's do it." If something is not right, you do the opposite by brushing off your shoulder or brushing off your sleeve as if something is on it. If you see the police or "Bunco Rollers" as they called them, again signal on your arm, making a rolling motion." She was told to rub her arm in a circular motion, and finally, the last and best signal you'll need to know is this: take your index finger and lightly touch your nose, moving your finger in an upward motion. This means everything is righteous… like the Mark just took her money out of the bank, and we're almost home! She was asked if she got all those instructions. Judith told me she was sure she could do it.

Over the next couple of weeks, they practiced in the apartment and even walked around in the streets looking at people discussing who and why they would pick or not pick a particular person. Judith told me that they knew she was a dope fiend, and she was out on the streets copping heroin not in a rich little neighborhood on Long Island but in Harlem on 128th Street and 8th Avenue they felt she must have some sort of an innate "slick sense" or "silver tongue."

She remembers the advise given to her: Your goal is simple. The game is simple. You do not need to be a rocket scientist to play this game, but you do need good intuition and street smarts. You need to pay attention to detail and be able to "turn on a dime" (adapt and think on your feet). You must be able to talk your way into, out of and around whatever comes up. Know the game and understand what part you are playing in that game. It is just like being an actor in a play. Memorize the script. Say your lines aloud and practice just like we've been doing. Do this and you are going to make money.

The first time she swindled someone (her first sting) she told me she felt terrible, but she was told she could not have done it unless they were greedy, which she knew was not true but, by that time, she knew how to manage bad feelings. Heroin would make those feelings melt away instantly. And Heroin, of course, does not disappoint she said. The guilty feelings disappeared and were replaced by the excitement of the sting and the money that she knew she was going to be able to make from then on.

She related a story to me about the time she and her partner, were working this Lame or Mark and when she opened the envelope and pulled the money up to flash, much to her surprise, not only were there no $100 dollar bills on the top and bottom, but even worse her partner at the time didn't use real dollar bills. Instead, she had used exactly what she was told not to use "play money." The envelope was stuffed with this bogus looking play money! Judith said the surprised look on her partner's face made her laugh aloud (she couldn't help herself) which made her partner start laughing. At which point, Judith said, she lost it and had tears running down her face from laughing so hard! She said to me that they played it off by her saying something like "Well, I hadn't fully opened or looked in the envelope and was just about to when I met you two." It was a ridiculous moment, stated by Judith. Like any job, you need to be prepared.

Somewhere buried under a bunch of drugs was the reality that although playing the game felt like an adventure, it was not a game. It was against the law and she was causing a huge problem in someone's life. Judith also understood that though money was the obvious reason for her excitement in the game, underneath it was something more sinister. The adrenaline rush (like a gambler gets) was, not surprisingly, yet another addiction she told me "People get addicted to coffee, not her she chose heroin and con games. Why she had to learn everything the hard way is something she still don't quite understand, but those choices are what got her here. Stealing people's money gave her bad memories, which made Judith feel extremely upset with herself. Everything in her life was wrong and she knew it. She explained "The problem is like so many things in life, you do it again... because you've done it before. You get up the next morning and just start all over again."

She had shot dope for close to 12 years and there were so many things she told me that she did wrong and so many people she hurt. She said she was ashamed, and I believed her. She was almost 30 years old, and by now had a 2-year-old child who on occasion wound up going in and out of those "get off houses" with her. She knew that either she was going to die (she told me she had already overdosed twice) or wind up in jail for a long time unless something radically changed.

As it turned out, I was her chance for a radical change! She said she remembered my eyes. When she met me the first time at the Triborough Bridge she liked my eyes. She said I had "kind eyes." OK. OK! She was a "sweet talker" but sometimes you gotta go with your gut and take a chance. Was it luck? Maybe. Was it intuition? I don't know...maybe. I like to think that it was the years on the job that gave me the experience to recognize truth over a con but whatever it was, she got the chance to change her life (which she did) and the Queens Confidence Team arrested and convicted a bunch of "felons." What can I say, that's what I call a "win-win"!

CHAPTER 4

CONNED THE CON

The New York State Courts ruled in the seventy's that law enforcement cannot enter someone's home without a warrant. This changed everything for law enforcement in the way we affected arrests. For years, if you had probable cause to affect an arrest you could enter a home and take someone in custody. This new law would delay, if not hamper arrests of criminals.

One day in the spring of 1973, Andy and I were investigating a completed Handkerchief Switch confidence scheme which netted the Stuff players $3,000. The victim or Lame was interviewed, giving a good description of the two Stuff players. As procedure, the Lame was asked to come to the office of the Queens Confidence Team, now located in the 112th Precinct to view photos. The Queens Confidence Team had established up-to-date photo files on confidence operators arrested in New York and from other states. The Lame after viewing photos, identified one of the two individuals that took his money as one, Robert Cox. The intelligence files created by Andy and me had listed his street name as "Bud." Checking our files on Bud we found his name with phone numbers taken from other confidence operators when they were arrested.

Andy and I had developed a relationship with the security department of the telephone company, to obtain with a subpoena subscriber information for the numbers listed under Bud. The phone company came back with addresses for those phone numbers, and we had to decide on which was correct. We decided to ride by the address of the latest home number (by date) and the others in our files and look at those locations before we tried to affect an arrest. After checking out the other addresses and the latest one we made a decision that the one address we had most recently should be the correct location for Bud. The information on the other addresses were old by years and we felt they were not valid locations for Bud. The phone number for this location appeared recently in the possession of persons previously arrested, we now felt we had the correct address of where Bud was residing.

The Queens District Attorney's office was reluctant to issue a warrant based on a photo identification or our intelligence file information. We explained this was probable cause to obtain the warrant and after his arrest we would place this individual in a line up to confirm he is the one responsible for the theft of the $3,000, which is a felony. This was not enough to convince the district attorney to issue a warrant. This now put us in a situation where we had to conduct a surveillance of the location and hope to see Bud leaving his residence. Based on the new law we could not enter the apartment and arrest Bud without this warrant. Surveillance is a time-consuming effort, which would take away from our other duties of investigations and street surveillance. We had to produce a solution to affect this arrest in a timely fashion before this individual relocated somewhere else.

The plan was to con the con. I would wear my NYPD uniform and use this as a ruse to get Bud out of his apartment to make the arrest without an arrest warrant. Confidence Operators are not afraid of uniform police officers but rather detectives, especially a Bunco Roller, who is trained in the conference field and specialized in these types of crimes.

Early one morning, Andy and I drove to the building in Harlem which is in Manhattan. Andy was stationed in the rear of the building in the event of an escape from the apartment. The back of the building is where the fire escapes came down from each floor. I went to the apartment located on fifth floor and knocked on the door hoping this was Bud's apartment. A man approached the door and asked, "Who is it?" I replied, "Police, I need to gain access to your apartment, someone is breaking in the apartment above you, and I need to get to the fire escape." The man opened the peep hole in the door and saw me in uniform. I continued to pound on the door. The man, later identified as Robert Cox, a.k.a. Bud, unlocked the door. I said to him, "Please come out for your safety." Seconds passed and finally, the man unlocked the door and stepped out into the hallway. After recognizing him as Bud, I informed him he was under arrest for the Stuff by Backstage and Soft-Shoes. After he was handcuffed, Bud stated," I cannot believe you conned me." Conned the con story would spread throughout the confidence community again adding to the reputation of Backstage and Soft-Shoes. Taking Bud into the 112th Precinct in uniform was a revelation for detectives working there. They could not believe I would put on my uniform to apprehend a felon. My comment was, "You do what you must." This individual was wanted on nine outstanding arrest warrants for other frauds committed throughout the City of New York. He was held without bail, and awaiting additional charges from those outstanding warrants. Lineups were scheduled for the nine victims to come to the Queens Confidence Team's office, located in the 112th Precinct.

The subject Bud was taken out of Rikers Island Detention Facility by a court order to stand in a lineup. Robert Cox was transported by Andy and I to the 112th precinct where the lineups were to take place. The assigned detectives accompanied their victims to view the lineup. Upon completion of the lineups and after obtaining positive identification of Bud, the detectives assigned went back to their respective district attorney for follow up court presentations. Grand Jury was the next step to indict Bud on these nine felonies.

This case like others, resulted in arrests, which came from information found in our intelligence files. This proved all our demanding work of maintaining those files paid off. Every bit of information saved can achieve an arrest of a subject in the future.

CHAPTER 5

SURVEILLANCE PAYS OFF

The Queens Confidence Team had been assigned to confidence game investigations for close to 5 years with over 300 arrests affected. Andy and I were still collaborating with our Informant on solving past cases in Queens and arresting wanted individuals on outstanding warrants. The Queens District Attorney was incredibly happy with the results and the number of indictments we made because of the cooperation of our Informant. This endorsement was important at the end of the day with trying to obtain probation for our Informant.

Over the past few weeks, we investigated swindles involving solo young female players. The victims of these swindles were unable to identify anyone from photos at the Pickpocket Confidence Squad or the Queens Confidence photo files. The Confidence Team's Informant called me and gave me valuable information she overheard in a conversation with a male subject named, "Slim." This individual had a string of young females in their early twenties who had been coached in how to pull, off the Drag swindles alone. The females came from out-of-state and had no criminal records. They are staying in an apartment in Queens. She also heard Slim joking about Backstage and Soft-Shoes in that he had Drag players living right under their noses in Queens. The female players would act alone, which was the new trend. Andy and I both felt they could be the players reported in the recent investigations in Queens of a solo female player.

The information we received on where these players were staying was a small apartment complex near the Grand Central Parkway on 112th Street in Corona, Queens. It was a quiet residential area with little traffic either on foot or in vehicles. A perfect location to hide people and not draw attention to them. The apartment complex oddly was named, the Surace Apartments, close to Backstages' last name, Farace. Watching the apartment front entrance would be a problem being this was a residential area. Two men sitting in an unmarked police car or van in an all-residential area would draw attention, which we did not want. Another plan had to be made on how Andy and I would keep this location under surveillance. We went around the corner to see what the back of this apartment building looked like. To our surprise, there was an ally leading from the back of the apartments to this street. If anyone entering or leaving was using this rear entrance, they would not be observed if we were positioned at the front entrance. Across from this ally were residential homes. We took a chance and rang the doorbell of the house directly across from the ally. The owner, an older gentleman let us in after we identified ourselves as detectives and showed our badges and police ID cards. The gentleman was being extremely cooperative and wanted to assist in any way he could. He lived alone and welcomed company. He was not concerned about us coming and going. His house was a perfect fit, it had a closed-in front porch, which we could use without interfering with the owner's privacy. The windows had blinds, which made it easier for us to lift slightly and view the comings and goings by way of this ally.

The next day both Andy and I, along with another detective who was assigned from the Queens Burglary Squad, went to the house directly across from the rear entrance of the Surace Apartments to start our surveillance. This detective on loan was an expert in the use of the 35 mm camera, which neither Andy nor I had at the time. We assumed a position inside the house while watching and photographing people leaving the apartment by this ally. It was closer to use the rear entrance than the front to get to the subway on Roosevelt Avenue. This first day was long with no actual results. The people leaving were older females who did not appear to be Drag players. The plan was if we saw a young female who looked good, Andy or I would follow on foot to determine if she was a player. Around 9 a.m. on the second day of surveillance, we observed a young attractive female leaving by way of this ally. Andy agreed to be the first to start foot surveillance and left the house shortly behind this female. In the seventy's, we did not have cell phones or portable radios to stay connected. Once Andy left, he was on his own. I lost sight of him as he turned the corner heading for the subway.

Hours passed while photos were taken of the comings and goings of individuals including men who could be involved in con games. The owner of the house handed me the phone. It was a call from Andy. He was up in the Bronx in the Precinct where he had arrested the solo female, he had been following earlier. Andy had taken the train with her up to the Grand Concourse in the Bronx where she approached an older woman on the street and started the Drag con game. Andy moved in and made the arrest. He did not tell the subject that he was Soft-Shoes in order not to blow our observations of the apartment back in Queens. He pretended he was a detective from that Precinct in the Bronx. The address the subject gave Andy when he was processing her was a bogus location in Manhattan. Andy knew this was false but never let on. He called me to inform me that he was on his way to the Bronx Criminal Court to process and charge this female prisoner.

At the arraignment later that evening, when her fingerprints came back, this female had no previous arrests. She appeared to be one of the young females from out-of-state as described earlier by our Informant. Andy was able to return the next day to join me at our observation location in Queens. Andy had appeared in court the night before and based on this female not having any prior arrests was released without bail for a future court appearance in a month or so. With the photo of the young female from Andy's arrest, it was now time to do a photo lineup of previous victims of solo players. One victim's description fit this female and the photo spread was shown to the victim by me later that day. The victim positively identified her as the one who had conned her out of $2,000 weeks earlier.

Surveillance was continued while I was away interviewing the past victim. Photos were taken of young women and men who were in and out of that apartment who looked good to Andy as players. Upon my return to the location, it was decided that I would follow the next suspected female player. The next day, we observed two young pretty females leaving the location together toward the train on Roosevelt Avenue. I left the observation location and followed them. This time they took me by train to Manhattan, to the Upper East Side. I kept the female suspects under observation. When one approached an elderly female, engaging her in conversation, the second female joined her, I moved in and took them into custody on an attempted fraud charge. I was able to flag down a passing marked radio car, which transported me and the female prisoners to the 17th Precinct for booking. Again, these females were led to believe I was a detective from the 17th Precinct and not Backstage. This ruse was working. Again, the two females were charged with a crime, had no previous arrest, and were released without bail for a future court appearance.

Traffic was heavy with people coming and going. After reviewing the developed photos from days prior, photos of two men looked like they could be players. It was decided if they emerged from the apartment Andy, and I would follow them. Having just said that the two men exited the building together. Andy and I went out of our location and saw them get into a vehicle parked down the street which had out-of-state license plates. Our car was parked nearby, and we followed the two in their vehicle. The subjects drove into Jamaica, parked their car, and started to walk on the street. After a short walk one approached a female in conversation and the second shortly thereafter joined them. Once we observed a handkerchief in the hands of one subject, we moved in and took the two into custody. They were attempting the Stuff con game or the better-known name, Handkerchief Switch. They were taken to the Queens Criminal Court after booking and charged with an attempted fraud. That evening they posted bail and were released pending a future court date. All this time these individuals and the three females had no idea they were being followed from the Surace Apartments. Our surveillance continued.

A call was made to our Informant who was asked to meet me and to view the surveillance photos taken over the past few days. It was hoped she could identify more individuals using this location as a base of operation. The Informant identified an elderly man later identified as Barry Smith, a known Handkerchief Switch Stuff player. A check on his arrest history revealed that he was wanted in other states including in New York City for past confidence game activity. Knowing this, we decided not to take him into custody until we had identified and or arrested all the other players living at that apartment location. Our investigation continued relative to the open cases where young females were involved. One of the other victims identified both of the females I had previously arrested in Manhattan. The female players had conned the victim out of $1,800. earlier this month. We would not affect an arrest of the two until we finished our surveillance operation.

After weeks of this surveillance, with hundreds of photos taken, we felt we had identified all who were living in this apartment building and who engaged in conducting confidence game swindles. A check on the previous arrests we made in the Bronx and Manhattan involving the young females, we came to find out they failed to appear in court. Bench warrants were issued for their arrests. This made rounding up these individuals easier being we now had arrest warrants for three subjects. Our arrests would make this a successful surveillance operation. It also identified the young females possibly being involved in other reported swindles in other boroughs or neighboring states. Their arrest photos were now available to be viewed by victims for identification.

Feeling comfortable that we had identified all the individuals living in this apartment building who were engaged in confidence games, a plan was set in motion to take all four individuals into custody at one time. Andy and I approached the building superintendent and asked for his cooperation.

The arrest photos were shown to him, he identified which apartments the females and one elderly con artist resided in. With a couple of detectives from the Burglary Squad, all the apartments were hit at the same time. We felt comfortable they were in those apartments because surveillance had not shown them leaving. We were successful, and arrested four individuals without incident, the three females and the one male. Back at the 112th precinct all four were being booked, the three females realized they had been conned by Backstage and Soft-Shoes after recognizing us as their arresting officers in both the Bronx and Manhattan. Again, our Informant had given us excellent information leading to the four arrests and the two other arrests for the Stuff con game.

The male individual, one Barry Smith was taken into custody on an old warrant and he now faced additional charges for the outstanding crimes for which he was wanted.

CHAPTER 6

AWARENESS AND TRAINING

In the beginning, Andy and I focused on stemming the flow of confidence games in the borough of Queens by affecting arrests. It was now time to take on an additional task of awareness training for seniors, the Queens banking industry, and the local press.

The borough commander in Queens was incredibly supportive of our success and suggested we approach the International Association of Chiefs of Police in Washington, DC and ask them to consider publishing an article on Confidence Games, in their monthly magazine. This police organization is comprised of members from all over the world. "The Police Chief" is their monthly publication and we were honored and accepted to place our story in this magazine. Our article appeared in the January 1975 addition. Having been recognized in the law enforcement community because of this article, we were now classified as experts during testimony at criminal trials and Grand Jury presentations. This gave us a tremendous advantage when we testified in court.

As part of the investigations and awareness information given by Andy and me, the victims are told of other means to swindle more money from the same victim. One incident that comes to mind after we met with a victim of the Stuff or the Handkerchief Switch. The victim was told that on occasion the con artist may pass on information about a score they made to individuals that would come back to the victim and pull off another fraud. The street term for this is "The Comeback." It is played by two men posing as detectives investigating a fraud. They show the victim phony badges and IDs to gain their confidence. Photos are also shown to the victim of the two individuals who had previously swindled her out of money stating, "We arrested them," and they admitted that the bank teller, where she withdrew her money, was involved. The subjects ask the victim to go to that bank again, see the same teller, and withdraw more money, which they will use as evidence. Once the victim complies thinking she is cooperating, the subjects take her money as evidence leaving a phony receipt for the cash and disappear. The victim was conned again.

In the fall of 1975, a female victim of the Stuff, Handkerchief Switch con game, who had been interviewed by Andy and me, had been briefed then of the follow-up con game, the Comeback. One day shortly after her loss, two men showed up at her home showing ID and a badge telling the victim they were investigating her case and had arrested the two con artists involved. They showed her photos of both individuals they said were arrested for stealing her money. The victim recalled what Andy and I had told her about a Comeback swindle, and she offered to help. She agreed to go to the bank to withdraw more money taking the two con men in her car toward the bank. Instead, she drove immediately to the 113th Police Precinct, jumped out of her car, and screamed for help. Uniform police officers grabbed the two and notified the Queens Confidence Team. Upon the arrival of Andy and I, we immediately seized the photographs of the two subjects, who they say were arrested. The photos would lead to their arrests for the original crime of the Stuff. This victim had pulled the wool over the con men's eyes.

Making arrests on the street and clearing past cases was the goal, but now we had to try to prevent those swindles from happening by bringing attention to all the local senior citizen facilities. In addition, we recruited the Queens banking sector to help educate their tellers on what to look for and assist in posting flyers at the actual bank locations to help prevent more swindles from occurring. We also tried to get more press coverage on arrests as an awareness tool. The first step for Andy and I was to write and develop lesson plans to use for lectures at senior citizen facilities in Queens. This task was assigned to Andy who was attending college working toward his master's degree. Andy had excellent writing skills and enjoyed public speaking even though the audience was older individuals who often fell asleep during his presentation. A blow to his ego. The next step was to reach out to the local banking association and set up a meeting to suggest our program to their board. Again, this task was assigned to Andy who loved this type of work. I would continue to focus my energy on maintaining the intelligence files. We had the freedom to schedule our shifts as needed. In a week, the tour would vary, days for surveillance on the street and court appearances, other days in the evening to interview past victims and try to resolve those cases and finally conduct training during business hours for the banks, with evenings for the senior presentations. Even though all this was happening, we still had time to affect arrests on the street, preventing the swindles from occurring.

The borough commander and the lieutenant in the burglary squad were always briefed on our weekly schedule for their approval. The one benefit we had was no real supervision, we had the option to do what was necessary. Results were always achieved, so there was no need to look over our shoulders on a daily or weekly basis. This was a great assignment to have in the detective division.

We needed to produce a way of educating the banking employees on what to look for. We talked to them at their morning meetings before the bank opened and developed a simple poster explaining the most common confidence game, the Pocketbook Drop or Pigeon Drop, also known as the Drag, which would be displayed on the banking floor. Andy and I reached out to the New York City Police Department's sketch artist. This individual would be called upon in exceptional cases to draw an image of a subject or subjects who were wanted for committing a serious crime. The team's request was out of the norm for the artist to do. Andy and I had an idea of four simple sketches showing the various steps of the Drag confidence game. Upon completion of the sketches, the NYPD Photo Unit took photos of the sketches and produced four small cartoon images we could use for our poster. Posters were made and now was the task of distributing them to the banks in Queens. We first had to get the assistance and permission of the bank's security directors to place them on the banking floors. This was another process of selling the idea to the banks and getting their cooperation. The neighboring police departments in Nassau and Suffolk Counties had an interest in our poster, to use as well as a crime prevention tool. Those police agencies went a step further and placed the poster in the Long Island newspaper for the public to see.

In 1976, The Honorable Mario Biaggi in the House of Representatives, was the Acting Chairman on the House Select Committee on the Aging. He was having a hearing in New York City on legislation to amend laws applying to the elderly. Andy and I representing the Queens Confidence Team were invited to give testimony at this hearing on the effect of confidence games on the elderly. In addition, the sergeant from the Pickpocket Confidence Squad was also asked to testify. This was a real honor for us to have been selected. Representative Mario Biaggi asked us if we could get one or two prior victims to come and testify for the record.

The House Select Committee on Aging was created under an act of Congress late in 1973. The purpose was to study and make legislative recommendations about problems and needs of America's 21 million (at that time) elderly. The hearing commenced with the Pickpocket and Confidence Squad sergeant testifying. Both Andy and I testified about the Pocketbook Drop. We spoke about their attempts to have a poster distributed to Social Security Offices to help reduce the crimes against the elderly. This request was refused by the Social Security Administration. Once the testimony concluded, Representative Biaggi stated he would follow up with the Social Security Agency to get an answer as to why they refused. Following both Andy's and my testimony, two Queens victims spent about 30 minutes telling their story about how Andy and I arrested the female subjects, and how one victim was lucky to get her money back through the court process. Unfortunately, we did not hear back from the committee regarding the Social Security Office accepting our poster. We also approached Utility companies to include a small flyer in monthly billing statements. This was also turned down. Today we receive in the mail many flyers along with our bills, we were ahead of the times back in the 70s.

CARTOON ILLUSTRATED FOR THE POSTER

CARTOON ILLUSTRATED FOR THE POSTER

CARTOON ILLUSTRATED FOR THE POSTER

CARTOON ILLUSTRATED FOR THE POSTER

CON ARTISTS AT WORK: The above police poster tells the story, of how people are being taken for large sums of money through the "envelope drop" con game. If you have been approached to participate in the racket, call police in Nassau at (516) 535-4244; in Suffolk at (516) 265-5000.

CHAPTER 7

PHONY TV SALE
MANHATTAN DA'S SQUAD

As the reduction of reported known confidence games decreased, the Confidence Team began to see new types of reported swindles. One major swindle in the seventies was the phony sale of VCR's and color TV sets at a reduced rate. The crimes were committed by opportunists depending on what was a high-priced product. Products like anti-freeze, TVs, and VCRs were in demand due to shortages with prices becoming extremely high.

One day in 1976, I received an anonymous call from a man who told me that a group of con artists were working out of a local bar on Main Street and Roosevelt Avenue in Jackson Heights, Queens. The pitch was televisions and anti-freeze at a discounted rate. They would tell the victim they were over-stocked goods at a department store or a hijacked tractor-trailer of TV sets they wanted to unload at a decent price. We began surveillance of the bar located on Main Street, which continued for weeks. Andy and I as part of our surveillance program would pass this location and make observations. This continued until one day we observed a group of four men standing outside the bar. We positioned ourselves across from the bar and continued to observe them. After a while, one of the four, the older man, began making phone call after phone call from a nearby pay phone. At this point, we knew exactly what they were doing. Unfortunately, Andy and I did not know who they were calling. This continued off and on for an hour. Eventually they all went back inside the bar. We broke off surveillance because the four men went back inside, which meant they were not successful in getting a victim to fall for the scheme.

Now that Andy and I knew we had a team of swindlers, surveillance started every day after that. It was not soon after we saw the four con men again making calls from the pay phone. This time it took only a couple of calls and they all walked over to a parked vehicle and got in. We followed their vehicle through parts of Queens and then into Manhattan. Eventually, they drove through the Holland Tunnel into New Jersey. We continued to follow them across state lines. All along the highway in New Jersey, they would pull over to a pay phone and make another call. They had a victim on the line who was falling for this fraud. Following the con men into another state was justified; the crime started in Queens, New York even though the possible victim was in New Jersey. After about three hours of surveillance, something must have happened, and the four con men turned around and headed back to Queens. It was possible the deal might have fallen through. Andy and I followed them back to the bar where they parked the vehicle and went back inside. This told us the swindle for today was over, and they would try another day. Armed with the con artist's license plate number, we identified the owner. A check under the owner's name revealed a previous arrest for a phony TV swindle. Now we knew they had a real case developing.

The on-and-off surveillance continued randomly until a week later when the four con men were observed again on the same pay phone. Currently, we did not have enough probable cause or evidence of a swindle to convince a district attorney to obtain a subpoena for the phone records from the pay phone. After only a couple of calls, they all went to the same vehicle and drove off toward Manhattan, although we thought they we are heading back to New Jersey. Once they went through the Queens Midtown Tunnel that thought changed. They parked their vehicle in a public parking garage in midtown Manhattan. The four walked towards 7th Avenue with Andy and I not far behind on foot.

On 7th Avenue, all four went into a Pizza restaurant. While inside the older man was observed again on the phone. Andy and I knew they had a victim nearby. It was not long before one of the four walked out of the restaurant leaving his three friends behind. I assumed foot surveillance of this one while Andy kept an eye on the other three individuals from a nearby restaurant. I observed the con artist I was following, standing on the corner waiting for someone. A brief time passed when a man approached the subject and engaged in conversation. This was the victim. The conversation continued for a while. I observed the male victim hand the con artist a white envelope. This was the norm for this type of swindle. This envelope contained money to purchase the goods, in this case, color TV's. I walked over to the con artist and the victim, identifying myself as a police officer, grabbed the subject, and was in the process of handcuffing him when at least ten individuals all with their weapons drawn pointing them at me, yelling Police! The victim was an undercover detective from the Manhattan District Attorney's Squad. I explained to the group of detectives that the subject was placed under arrest for a confidence game. The detectives at that point did not have a clue what was happening.

The undercover detective took the place of a victim who called the Manhattan District Attorney's office informing them about a call he received about purchasing a tractor-trailer load of stolen color TV sets. The undercover officer had the bills marked for evidence and was wearing a wire to record the conversation between him and the subject once they recovered the tractor-trailer. I immediately told the detective in charge, a sergeant, that three others were involved, and my partner had them under surveillance on 7th Avenue. Immediately, everyone went back to the restaurant and met Andy who pointed out the subjects who were arrested and taken into custody without incident. The sergeant told Andy and me to meet them at the Manhattan District Attorney's office in Lower Manhattan to sort this situation out. The district attorney detectives transported the subjects to their office. At the office, Andy and I met with the captain to explain what was happening. It was apparent the detectives in this squad had no idea this was a confidence game and there was no tractor-trailer loaded with stolen color TV sets to purchase. This was like the movie, "The gang that couldn't shoot straight." The district attorney's squad deployed extensive resources to this case, convinced they had a hijacked load of color TV sets. After explaining how this works, the squad members were embarrassed that they fell for the fraud. I explained Andy and I had these individuals under observation for weeks, following them that day from Queens to Manhattan. The original call to the victim was in Queens where the crime started. The captain agreed and at the end of the day, the detectives now understood what a confidence game is all about, the hard way.

Frauds of this type continued in both the Bronx and Queens using local Korvette Department Stores as the place to pick up the color TV sets or the VCR's. Even though the arrest Andy and I made was in the Bronx, the crime started with a call to the victim in Queens. On occasions, we affected arrests in that borough and transported the subjects back to Queens for prosecution. On one occasion, the victim was instructed to bring his truck to the loading platform at Korvette's in Queens to pick up the TV's. The victim was reluctant to meet the subject, so I took his place. I could drive a stick shift. I drove the victim's truck to the store and waited to be approached. It was not long after backing the truck into the loading bay area that I was approached by a man, who told me he worked for Korvettes. I handed the con artist the envelope containing marked bills. Once he took the envelope, I placed him under arrest. Andy had observed this con artist drive up with an accomplice. That individual was also taken into custody. After a couple of years passed, this confidence swindle was played out and stopped. All this time we, still focused on the day-to-day con games occurring with the help and cooperation of our Informant making on average seven arrests a month.

CHAPTER 8

DRAG SOLO PLAYER

After years of working on confidence games, Andy and I had a case reported to us by an elderly woman who lived in Jamaica, Queens. Her complaint was about a young female who had stayed over in her house and eventually stole $20,000 and her jewelry which the young woman (a Drag con girl) manipulated her to withdraw from her local bank. Typically, two or three players would play the Drag confidence game, all acting as if they were strangers to convince the victim, the Lame, to participate in the swindle. This was the first time that we encountered a solo Drag player operating, what we call a Sleepover swindle.

The victim reported to the police that she met this young woman on the street in Jamaica late in the afternoon who showed her a canvas bag that she claimed she found on the street. When opened, inside appeared to be a considerable sum of money. The Drag girl asked if she could go to the victim's apartment and use her phone to call an attorney for advice on what to do with the bag. After the call, the Drag girl told the elderly victim that she needed to show a sign of good faith by putting up her own money. In return, she would share in the found money, allegedly $70,000. Realizing the time of day, and the fact that the victim's bank was now closed, the young woman asked to stay over and go to the bank early the next day. The victim agreed. The next morning, they went to the victim's bank, opened her safe deposit box, and took out $20,000 in cash and her jewelry, valued around $3,000. This was placed into a second bag the Drag girl had with her for safekeeping and to show the attorney. They proceeded to walk to a nearby office building taking the second bag with the victim's money and jewelry and went up to see the attorney. The victim waited downstairs. The Drag girl came back down and now had two bags, one containing her share of the found money and the other had the $20,000 in cash and her jewelry the victim just took out of the safe-deposit box. They both went back to the bank and the victim placed both bags into her safe-deposit box without looking inside the bags. The alleged attorney advised the young woman and the Lame to safeguard this money for a couple of days to see if anyone comes forward to claim the lost bag of cash. At this point, the Drag girl left, and the victim went home.

Later that morning the victim was curious and went back to the bank to open her safe-deposit box. When she opened the box, the canvas bag and the second bag with her share of the found money, contained cutup paper with no money or jewelry. At this point, the victim realized she had been conned and went to the police. The Drag girl had switched the bags when she saw the alleged attorney. The Confidence Team was notified by the local police precinct of this fraud and responded, arriving at the victim's apartment to conduct the investigation. This was the largest confidence fraud we encountered since we started years earlier. The amount of money taken was well above the normal take on this type of swindle. In the 70's, the norm was from $1,500 to $3,000. This was the first time the Confidence Team had an actual crime scene to examine. Most, if not all confidence games are committed on the street and in public places. The victim being extremely upset was on the phone with her doctor when Andy and I arrived at her apartment. The doctor prescribed medication to help reduce her stress. She had lost all her savings. We asked if she had a bank account, and she informed us that she did not like bank accounts preferring cash, which she kept in her safe-deposit box.

The interview took a couple of hours, going over every minute that the victim could remember, including a detailed description of the Drag girl. She told me that the Drag girl had made a couple of phone calls from her apartment, one to the attorney and one to her family telling them she was okay, and that she was staying with a friend overnight. The Confidence Team now had leads to follow up on at the victim's apartment. With the victim's permission we contacted the phone company to retrieve the numbers called from the victim's home the prior night. Forensic examination of the apartment for fingerprints was conducted and a review of the bank surveillance cameras to see if an image of the young female subject was captured. As luck would have it, the savings bank had surveillance camera issues that day and no images were found of the subject. Both Andy and I were proficient in lifting fingerprints as we had special training as part of the Burglary Squad. Examination of the victim's apartment, especially in the bathroom and in the kitchen were dusted and latent fingerprints were found. The victim had not cleaned up the dishes and glasses they used the night before which were still in the sink. The glass was dusted for prints with latent fingerprints found. The prints were lifted and saved as evidence. The victim was printed for elimination purposes. All the lifted fingerprints were vouchered as evidence as part of this investigation. In addition, the two bags containing the cut-up paper were vouchered.

Phone company records revealed there were two calls made to the same phone number during the evening hours the night before. A later check on these numbers showed it to be a pay phone located on 7th Avenue and 122nd Street in New York City. This area was known for Pickpockets and Confidence operators frequented. A check of this phone number through our intelligence file found individuals calling that same number. It was a good lead to follow up on to conduct surveillance on this location and attempt to take photos of those using the phone. Unfortunately, we did not have the time to devote to this being our team was only two people and busy with surveilling and conducting other investigations. In the future, Andy and I could devote time to gathering more intelligence on the Confidence operators from that location.

The latent fingerprints lifted by us were submitted to the NYPD Latent Fingerprint Unit for comparison. Unfortunately, there was no hit. Either this Drag girl had not been arrested in New York or lived out of state with no criminal history. Our next step was to drive the victim to police headquarters to view photos of known female confidence operators at the Pickpocket Confidence Squad office in hopes of identifying the person who stole her money and jewelry.

The Pickpocket and Confidence Squad maintains a massive number of photos of those arrested for con games. The victim viewed photos of females, but no identification was made. This was a young female who had never been arrested. The Pickpocket Squad acknowledged they had no other reports of a single Drag female pulling off such a large score. Driving the victim back to her Queens apartment, we advised her of another swindle, the Police Comeback, and the Bank Auditor swindle. We explained to the victim that she could be approached at home by men identifying themselves as detectives or bank auditors. The victim would be told that the bank teller or the safe deposit manager was involved. They would show the victim a Polaroid photo of the female subject stating she was arrested and now they need her help to arrest the person at the bank who was involved. The con artist will ask her to go back to the bank and take out more money. Once she did this, they would take this money as evidence and go back and arrest the teller or safe deposit box area manager. Being the victim told us that was all the money she had; this would not happen, we hoped. The victim was given my home number being I was assigned to this investigation. She was told I would be the only law enforcement person involved in this investigation and if she had any questions, to call me.

Over the next few weeks, I received a daily call from the victim asking if I had gotten her money and jewelry back. With no other leads to pursue, I reached out to the team's Informant. Judith was asked to find out anything on the street being discussed about this score. This was a major case in Queens and one that the Queens DA was interested in solving. It would be good publicity for the DA's office. The DA's representative was briefed on our progress and informed him we were now seeking help from our Informant, Judith the one they agreed to release from jail to assist the Confidence Team. A couple of days went by before we heard back from our Informant. The word on the street was a con artist, street name "Bread" was responsible, and he had just purchased a new brown Cadillac Coup Deville. He used the proceeds from the score to purchase the vehicle. The only other information she had was that the Drag girl was staying in an apartment on Tiebout Avenue in the Bronx. Also, the con artist known as Bread was living somewhere on the Grand Concourse in another apartment in the Bronx. A check of the Queens Confidence Intelligence file showed street names listed such as Bread, Stale Bread, and Short Bread, all having phone numbers. Based on this information, we approached the Queens District Attorney's office and spoke to the DA to help with any legal issues we needed to resolve this case. We obtained a subpoena for the phone records of the numbers we had in the confidence file to try and locate an accurate location for the con artist, Bread, the person who was behind this score. This would take days to get the information from the telephone company. This information was invaluable and a good start of the Informant's cooperation.

Andy and I briefed the lieutenant and borough commander on what we found and our next steps. To start, we would conduct surveillance of the building on Tiebout Avenue to try and identify the Drag girl while we waited for the phone company records. We could then develop a case against the con artist Bread. The apartment building on Tiebout Avenue was a six-story building with many apartments. The location was exceedingly difficult to surveil even using a closed van. The summer heat would be a factor, which would make sitting inside a closed van impossible. So, Andy and I opted to try to get an apartment location across the street from the entrance to the Tiebout Avenue address to set up surveillance. Luck has it, an apartment on the 3rd floor in a building across from the entrance to the Tiebout Avenue location was unoccupied. This gave us a perfect line of sight of the entrance to the Tiebout Avenue location. After conferring with the DA assigned, it was decided that photographs of all the females entering and leaving this location would be taken. The intent was to get a photo that the victim could identify as the female who had conned her, thus giving the Confidence Team probable cause to arrest her. Both Andy and I were not trained in using a 35-millimeter camera to take surveillance photos.

I spoke with the lieutenant in the Burglary Squad and asked again for another detective, the same one who helped us on a previous case, to be assigned to take photos at the Tiebout Avenue location. The lieutenant approved this, and we then briefed the Detective on what we were looking for, which included a brown Cadillac Coup Deville. Andy and I approached the building manager and we were able to get his permission to use the unoccupied apartment for the surveillance. The detective set up his tripod and camera and started the surveillance. He also brought his lunch and a cooler. His hours, for now, started at 0700 until 1800 and he was instructed to remain at that location alone.

Myself, a.k.a. Backstage, and my partner, Detective Camera, a.k.a. Soft-Shoes, would not be at that location during the surveillance. We would continue surveilling the streets and conduct other investigations in Queens. Every few days I would go up to the Tiebout Avenue location to pick up the rolls of film from the detective. Once the film was developed, the photos were sorted for identification. This went on for two weeks when one day the detective contacted me with information that he photographed a brown Cadillac Coup Deville that had just pulled up at the location. He was able to get the license plate number, which was from the State of Alabama. He also was able to get a photo of the male driver, who we believed was the con artist, Bread. This was great news, as we now had leads to follow-up on. We know con artists use out-of-state license plates with bogus addresses. That would not help with this case, but the photo of Bread would for sure. The surveillance went on for days when the detective called saying he thought the photo he took of a young female leaving that location could be our subject. After developing the film, we had a clear close-up shot of a young female fitting the description the victim gave us earlier.

A photo spread of young females was shown to the victim. Without hesitation the victim identified this female as the one who stayed over in her apartment and stole her money. Having this identification, we decided to take her into custody hoping to gain a confession and admission of Bread's involvement. This would lock in a conspiracy charge against Bread. Andy and I stayed put across the street from the Tiebout Avenue address, waiting for the suspect to appear. Shortly after setting up in the location, she exited the building. Andy and I identified ourselves as Backstage and Soft-Shoes placing her under arrest. The suspect, later identified as Angela Perez a.k.a. Mary Tilson, age 22, was transported back to the 112th Precinct in Queens to be booked on a felony charge of grand larceny. At the precinct she was fingerprinted, with a copy of her prints driven over to the Latent Fingerprint Bureau at Police Headquarters to compare against the fingerprints lifted in the victim's apartment. Within minutes the prints were confirmed a match. Now Andy and I had a solid case for prosecution. The district attorney assigned to the team advised us to wait until we conducted an interview with Ms. Perez before he prepared the court affidavit. Back at the 112th Precinct, I sat in the interview room with the subject, Ms. Perez. I explained the case to her and that she is facing at least 5-7 years in prison for this felony charge, which was based on the victim's identification and more importantly her fingerprints being found inside the victim's apartment. Ms. Perez became cooperative and offered to help to avoid a heavy jail sentence. She indicated she knew Bread as one Larry Ogletree. She gave me an address on the Grand Concourse in the Bronx where Mr. Ogletree was living. Oddly, this address was in our intelligence file. We received information from the phone company on the phone numbers we asked them to check, which confirmed the same information we had in our files.

The following day, Andy and I went to the Grand Concourse location and observed the brown Cadillac parked nearby. We placed the vehicle under surveillance and soon a male subject, later identified as Larry Ogletree approach the vehicle. As he opened the door of the car and was about to start it, he was placed under arrest. We seized the Cadillac as proceeds of the crime taking the car along with Larry Ogletree back to the 112th Precinct for booking on a felony charge of grand larceny. I drove the Cadillac to my home before bringing it to the police pound. The intent was to use the Cadillac as a psychological tool on the street at various locations where known confidence operators gathered. After obtaining a search warrant for the apartment of Angela Perez, the victim's jewelry was recovered and vouchered as evidence. The following morning, I, Backstage and Andy, Soft-Shoes drove the Cadillac to Harlem in New York to a local restaurant, Angela's Kitchen located on 7th Avenue, now known as Adam Clayton Powell Blvd and 122nd Street. Confidence operators and pickpockets used this location to eat and meet other criminals. Andy and I drove up in the brown Cadillac parking right in front of the restaurant. There were people on the street by this location who were shocked to see two white males who they knew were the police get out of Bread's car. One man on the street approach Andy and I and stated, "This is Bread's car." I replied, "No this is now Backstage and Soft-Shoe's car."

We went inside and had eggs without a sound from the others who were also eating. The reputation of Backstage and Soft-Shoes was enhanced even more with this act. We kept the Cadillac for a week using it on patrol until we turned it into the police pound. Angela Perez and Larry Ogletree were charged in Queen's criminal court and held pending grand jury action. The victim, along with myself appeared at the grand jury with an indictment for grand larceny being handed down on both individuals.

A trial date was set a month away. The success of this investigation was achieved with the help of our registered Informant, Judith who gave us the leads to solve this case. In addition, the cooperation of the Queens District Attorney's Office, the Latent Fingerprint Unit, and surveillance photographs helped seal this case. The victim was not happy that we did not recover her money, but we did get back her jewelry valued at $3,000. The Cadillac, even though it was the proceeds of this crime was held pending the outcome of the case. Later, the victim could seek to get the vehicle sold and the money refunded to her. The daily calls I was receiving from the victim finally stopped.

CHAPTER 9

THE GYPSY SWINDLE

It is estimated there are one million Romani people in the United States. They are also known as American Gypsies. The term Gypsy is considered a racial slur, used because of their lifestyle of moving from place to place and making money through unstandardized methods. As early as 1887, a man named Mr. J. Wood Wright allowed a full-blown Gypsy encampment to set up shop on his property on Broadway and 173rd Street as part of a charity event to raise money for Manhattan Hospital. It was one of the first experiences for the public to see how their culture dressed and their crafty maneuvers with fortune-telling and other spiritual cons. A real Gypsy camp sat on the meadows between Broadway, Harlem River between 211th and 212th Streets. Despite this outpouring of acceptance, the freewheeling days of Gypsies setting up camp on the farms and pastures of this turn of the century were drawing to a close. By 1904, Gypsy camps would become all but impossible to exist. Today a close-knit group of approximately 350 Gypsy families live in the Bronx who are proud of their culture and traditions. They are wary of discrimination and stereotypes, with letting people assume they are Italian or Greek.

The Queens Confidence Team had limited involvement in investigating Gypsy confidence game cases. Most people who were swindled never reported them to the police. Andy and my interaction with Gypsies were mostly through observations while on street surveillance and roaming. Across the country there are Tarot Card reading locations, storefronts, or small houses operated by Gypsies. Individuals go to the locations to seek help and advice. The victims are people who have personal issues, family or health related. The Gypsy charges a fee for a Tarot Card reading giving her the opportunity to size up a person. Once they realize the victim has wealth, they perform the Gypsy blessing, known to them as a Bajour or Blessing con game. This swindle involves a curse on a person's wealth. The Gypsy would tell them to get rid of this curse, their money must be burned. The victim brings in cash, which is placed in an envelope or handkerchief and burned. Prior to burning, the victim is distracted, and the envelope or handkerchief is switched to one with just paper. This could go on for months and years.

In the late 70's, there was a major problem in New York with foreign born Gypsies who participated in house burglaries and assaults on the elderly more than just con games. Most Gypsies living in the U.S. engaged in Tarot Card readings and the Bajour/Blessing confidence game. The most important person in the Gypsy world are the females. They are the money makers doing Tarot Card readings and con games. The men do minor frauds, body and fender work, and coating home driveways.

Although house burglaries were not part of the mandate for the Queens Confidence Team, we were aware of what was occurring on the residential streets. As Andy and I rode the streets looking for Drag and Stuff players, we also had in the back of our minds the violent Gypsies.

Recently reported to the police was a homicide in the Flushing area of Queens, New York, where a female Gypsy knocked on the door of an elderly woman seeking a glass of water. She pretended to be pregnant. The elderly woman let her in and the two went to the kitchen to get a glass of water. Once they were away from the front door, the male counterpart would enter to ransack the house. Unfortunately, the elderly women heard this and confronted the male. He grabbed her, tied her up, using a rag to cover her mouth. He then placed the elderly woman in a closet and fled. This woman suffocated in that closet and was found by her daughter later in the afternoon that same day. An Investigation by detectives assigned to this homicide were able to find a witness who saw two individuals in a vehicle with out-of-state license plates near the victim's home on the day of the incident. An alarm for that vehicle was transmitted and a marked radio car spotting the vehicle a brief time later. They were apprehended and placed into custody.

The two Gypsies were born in Europe and hardly spoke any English. Even though the two were arrested, burglaries and thefts continued without anyone else being harmed.

In another incident, while Andy and I were roaming through the Richmond Hills area of Queens, we observed a vehicle with three occupants. They drove slowly through a residential area and finally stopped near 149th Street and South Conduit Avenue. We kept their vehicle under surveillance, after a couple of minutes a female exited and walked toward a nearby home. She rang the doorbell, and an elderly woman opened the door. After about five minutes of conversation, the Gypsy went inside with the woman. At this point, the male Gypsy exited the vehicle, approached the front door, and went inside. Andy and I jumped out of our car and entered the house, placing the male and female Gypsies under arrest. The elderly woman was not injured. Still sitting in the vehicle was a 16-year-old girl who was also taken into custody and charged as a co-conspirator. The investigation of the three arrested, based on their description and how they operated, it was believed they had engaged in eight other robberies and burglaries in the same area of Astoria and Glendale in Queens, New York.

All the Gypsy families know one another. While I was on vacation in Tunica, Mississippi after retiring, I observed a large group of Gypsies in the hotel where I was staying. It appeared to me they were having a gathering of families. I went outside and saw dozens of autos with out-of-state license plates parked near the hotel entrance. I took down license plate numbers from states across the country and went back inside the hotel to call the local police. To my surprise, the police were not interested in this gathering. Having so many Gypsies from across the country in one place would be a major source of intelligence information. Hotel records could have been checked to see the names of who was checked in. This reminded me of the Appalachia Mafia gathering in upstate New York of the five crime families operating in that state and across the country. Lacking a specialist to investigate, confidence games in and around the Tunica area was a definite disadvantage and a loss of a real intelligence opportunity. The few days I stayed at the casino I was never exposed to so many Gypsies in one place. I always had my hand on my wallet.

CHAPTER 10

BARBARA ST. JAMES INVESTIGATION

My partner Andy and I are still collaborating with our Informant on solving past cases in Queens and other boroughs as well as locating and arresting wanted individuals on outstanding warrants. The Queens District Attorney's office has been pleased with Andy and my results and the number of indictments we presented to the grand jury. The indictments came as a direct result of information from and cooperation of our Informant, Judith.

In the fall of 1977, a full-page story was printed in the New York Daily News on the Pocketbook Drop Confidence Game. Featured in this article was a female known by the name of Barbara St. James, just one of her aliases that police records have under her fingerprints. A major Pocketbook Drop or Pigeon Drop score was made in the fall of 1976 in Fort Lee, New Jersey, which netted the Drag team $30,000. As the

117

years have gone by, the scores were increasing and this was a major case for the Fort Lee Police Department, which they had to solve. Their victim had identified Barbara St. James from photos as one of the con artists that took her money. The second Drag female player was not identified. A New York City Police Department check under the name of Barbara St. James disclosed wanted cards based on that name and other aliases used by her. Included, was one outstanding bench warrant in Queens, New York. This warrant goes back about seven years, which was prior to the formation of the Queens Confidence Team. This bench warrant was issued for a felony confidence game charge when she failed to appear in court to answer those charges. The Pickpocket and Confidence Squad was contacted and additional information from that squad told Andy and I this female was responsible for other major crimes across the county, including Toronto, Canada. The Pickpocket Squad consider her to be one of the most wanted Drag females due to the large scores she was making and the fact she has not been apprehended for years. To Andy and I this was a good opportunity to evaluate our Informant once again to see if we can learn any information from her on the where-a-bouts of Barbara St. James. The fact that Canadian authorities also wanted her could mean she is living in Canada.

Andy and I approached the Queens District Attorney's office to get their assurance if the team found her, they would prosecute her even if she were apprehended out of the country. This case, if solved with her arrest, would give the Queens DA press coverage for him and for his office. The

Informant, Judith was contacted, and a meeting took place where I showed her the newspaper article with the images of Barbara St. James. Judith told me that she knew her but under another name, Susan Adams. At this point, she was not sure where the subject was living and needed time to check further. The Informant was told, solving this case would help her tremendously at the time of sentencing on her case in Nassau and the others from out-of-state. The newspaper article back in 1977, the one that drew the attention of Andy and I at the time, the press referred to Barbara St. James "If you meet her, you will like her. She will draw out your life story, your troubles, and triumphs. She appears wealthy, a women of substance and class. She drips with sincerity." No other information about Barbara St. James is discussed. The reference in this news article gives St. James the air of being someone special and able to rip people off for big scores, which was proven by the swindles that she completed across the country.

Since the inception of the Queens Confidence Squad there was always competition between the Pickpocket Confidence Squad and us. Andy and I received fair amount of press coverage on our arrests. Andy and I affecting this arrest of Barbara St. James would be a feather in our cap. Days passed and finally I received a call from Judith. The information on Barbara St. James a.k.a. Susan Adams, was that she is living in Toronto. This was all she knew so far but would still try to locate an address for her. With this information, a call was placed to the district attorney assigned to Andy and me on this case. The DA was brought up to speed on our progress. The DA was standing by to prepare a warrant for Barbara St. James once we had an address in Canada. Within two days, Judith reached out to me with an address in Toronto, Canada. I immediately got on the phone with the Toronto Police Services Department and the Royal Canadian Mounted Police and had a discussion with them seeking their help in apprehending this subject. The DA was called who also reached out to those departments and assured them that the Queens District Attorney's office would extradite her back to the U.S. to face charges. Following those calls, the Toronto Police Services agreed to surveil this location and take her into custody. In the meantime, the DA's office was preparing the necessary paperwork for extradition. The Toronto Police Services Department set up surveillance and watched the comings and goings of this location, which was an apartment complex. Andy and I sent the photos via express mail to the police of Barbara St. James to assist them in identifying her and affecting the arrest. No sooner than having this conversation with the Toronto Police, Judith called me again. This time she told me that Susan Adams, a.k.a Barbara St. James was out of the country in Mexico. She was coming back from Acapulco arriving at Kennedy Airport (now JFK). Andy and I went to the DA's office with the updated information. Two detectives from the District Attorney's squad were assigned to go with Andy and I to Kennedy Airport.

Protocol was to inform the Port Authority Police Department that four armed detectives would be on the property at Kennedy

(JFK) Airport to make an arrest. The Port Authority assigned two uniform police officers to assist the four of us. The flight landed and as the passengers were exiting the plane, Barbara St. James was identified. She was taken into custody. Ms. St. James was transported back to the Queens DA's office for processing on the outstanding bench warrant. The name she gave to Andy, and I was Randee Brodsky, which was a new alias with an address of 213 East 64th Street, New York, NY. No one during the arrest mentioned to her the address in Toronto. The Toronto Police were notified that Ms. St. James was in custody and were thanked for all their assistance in this investigation. Now that Barbara St. James was in custody came the task of setting up lineups for all the victims in New York and the one from Fort Lee, New Jersey. The victims were asked to come to Police Headquarters and try to identify her as the con artist that stole their money. In all, the total of money allegedly taken by Ms. St. James was close to $90,000. The lineup was successful, and victims identified her. A warrant was lodged against her from the Fort Lee Police Department on their $30,000 case.

As a result of this arrest, the lieutenant of the Pickpocket Confidence Squad called the Queens borough commander and made a request to have Andy and I transferred to his unit in Manhattan, giving us the entire City of New York to patrol at our leisure. This was a big decision for Andy and me to leave Queens and transfer to Manhattan. Even though both of us lived on Long Island, we could sign in from Queens and not be required to go into the office at Police Headquarters in Manhattan. The borough commander recognized that the confidence game cases were reduced and could be managed by the local detective districts and did not object to this transfer. The decision was for Andy and me to make. Being part of the oldest and longest active squad in New York City Police Department's history was an honor. After discussing this transfer, we decided to try working in that unit and accepted the transfer.

This was a new experience working in a unit with other detectives and under supervision, to the point of telling us where to patrol and what to focus on. It was not going well for Andy and me. All the work we did on our intelligence gathering did not continue and was not accepted by the unit or the detectives assigned. This was really disappointing to us who spent so much of our time over the seven years putting it all together and keeping it updated. The value of this file was not appreciated. We believed it was a valuable tool to use which would help solve cases in the future. At the same time, by coincidence, the police department was under pressure to investigate major financial frauds that were occurring. With the introduction of computers, frauds were out of control, millions were being lost to Ponzi schemes and other financial frauds. The department made the decision to change the name of Pickpocket Confidence Squad to the Financial Frauds Squad, thus eliminating the longest detective squad in the history of the Police Department. As part of this change, a reduction of detectives was initiated, instead of being increased due to budget issues. The city was going through tough times and did not have money, to the point of borrowing money from the police pension funds to keep operating. Andy and I were the last in and the first to go. This was a sigh of relief to us as we were not happy working in the environment of the squad and welcomed again a transfer.

I, a.k.a. Backstage, and Andy, a.k.a. Soft-Shoes would start a new chapter in our police careers after giving up confidence game surveillance and investigations. Andy was assigned to special prosecutor Maurice Nadjari's task force conducting confidential investigations regarding corruption in the government operations of New York. He remained there for one year and retired as a Detective Second Grade continuing to a career with the Brooklyn Union Gas Company. I was assigned to the First Homicide Squad and then ultimately transferred to The Major Case Squad in Police Headquarters and then to the NYPD/FBI Joint Bank Robbery Task Force, where I worked until retirement in 1987 close to 24 years as a Detective Second Grade. I joined the Investment Bank, JP Morgan and worked there for 15 years, retiring as a Managing Director of Corporate Global Security for the firm.

CHAPTER 11

NEWS STORIES AND IMAGES

Racket gets a Spanish accent

Police grab 3 in Queens flim-flam

By IRVING LONG   7/22/74

Detectives from the Queens Confidence Team of the city Police Department arrested a 26-year-old South American man yesterday on charges of trying to flim-flam a deceased Corona woman.

Detectives said they had been looking for the suspect for about six months. He was identified as Juan Parra, 26, a resident of an upper Manhattan hotel. Arrested with him were Alberto Anciver, 25, and Louis Gonzales, 26, both South American aliens and residents of Manhattan hotels. They were arrested in Flushing by Detectives Andrew Camera and Theodore Farace, both of the Queens Confidence Team, under the supervision of deputy chief Edwin Droter.

Police estimated similar swindles have cost a number of Corona residents thousands of dollars in recent weeks.

Handkerchief switch still sells suckers   7/73

Three Queens detectives assigned to look for "confidence men" operating in the Jamaica area, yesterday arrested two suspects attempting to pull "the old handkerchief switch" on an unwary shopper.

Detectives Andy Camera and Ted Farace of the 16th District Burglary Squad and Detective George Bartlett of the Pickpocket Squad, all assigned to special confidence game surveillance, said the suspects Sivan Davis, 36, and Haywood Attmore, 34, both from Manhattan, were arrested after the officers observed them trying to switch an unidentified shopper around 2 p.m. near the intersection of Merrick Blvd. and Jamaica Ave.

Both Davis and Attmore were charged with fraudulent accosting for illegal purposes and loitering, and were arraigned last night in Kew Gardens Criminal Court. Fraudulent accosting is a Class A misdemeanor and, if convicted, the two could receive maximum sentences of up to a $1,000 fine and one year in jail.

Farace and Camera said they were assigned to cover the Pickpocket Squad confidence men with the Pickpocket Squad because of a rash of reported swindles in recent weeks, totalling over $250,000 "taken mostly from senior citizens." In the last two weeks, the three detectives have made at least nine "con game" arrests.

They said yesterday's attempted swindle was a classic example of the "Handkerchief Switch."

2 gals arrested again on conning elderly out of $ 12/73

Two housewives were arrested for the second time in 10 days yesterday for their alleged part in a confidence game which has victimized elderly Queens residents.

Charged with five additional counts of grand larceny were Mrs. Carolyn Arms, 27, of 70 W. 95th St., Manhattan, and Mrs. Anita Madkins, 31, of 2332 Tiebout Ave., Bronx. Both were arraigned in Queens Night Courth, Kew Gardens.

According to memb...

'Pocketbook drop' game thwarted, 2 women held

By STEVE LETZLER   7/25/74

Two detectives assigned to the Queens Confidence Team thwarting the alleged $500 "pocketbook drop" game...

2 Women Arrested On Con Game Charge   7/26/1972

Two young Manhattan women were arrested in Queens yesterday on charges of trying to bilk an elderly woman with the "envelope" confidence scheme, police reported.

The arresting officers were Detectives Andrew Camera and Ted Farace of the 16th Detective District, who were assigned to a special con...

Long arm of the law tags elusive target   4/23/76

A man wanted by police as the alleged operator of numerous con games was arrested by Queens detectives yesterday.

Police said the man, Robert Cox, 27, of Manhattan, has seven outstanding warrants against him and is being investigated for possible involvement in 24 incidents totaling $25,000 throughout the city.

Queens Detectives Andrew Camera and Theodore Farace, attached to the confidence game unit of the Queens Burglary Squad, made the arrest yesterday after Farace posed as a uniformed officer looking for a prowler in Cox's apartment building and convinced the man to open the door.

The arrest climaxed an investigation which had been conducted for several weeks under the direction of Sgt. Fred Dielensnyder of the Queens Burglary Squad, following the complaint of a Jamaica woman reportedly conned out of several thousand dollars in the "handkerchief switch" game.

Farace and Camera had received a tip as to Cox's

whereabouts, and they had staked out the five-story building where he was living for several weeks before they finally moved in yesterday.

According to police, the handkerchief switch involves two con men and a victim.

One man often poses as a naive seaman just arrived in New York. He approaches a victim and tells him (or her) that he is looking for a hotel, which invariably is little known or does not exist. In explaining his problem, he pulls out a slip of paper with the name of the hotel on it, along with a seemingly large wad of money, which is predominantly phony.

When the victim cannot direct the con man, they call a second man, passing by, who is the con man's partner. The same procedure is repeated with him, but the con man's partner cautions the "naive" man about carrying around so much money, and urges him to put it in a bank.

The con man replies he doesn't like banks because

they don't give the money back, and says he has been paying the captain of his ship or someone else to hold his money.

The con man's partner in trying to persuade him to put his money in the bank, and the victim is offered a large sum of money simply to withdraw money from his own account to show the "dumb sailor" that the money is, in fact, returned.

After the victim withdraws the money, the sailor thanks him and says he wants the victim to hold his money while he gets the rest from his captain so he can bank it. Both sums are then put into a handkerchief and given to the victim, who usually puts it in his pocket, or in the case of a woman, her purse.

One of the men then objects, and says money should be kept elsewhere, and takes back the bundle, shows the victim how to hide the bundle, then hands it back. It is usually then that the switch is made, and the victim is left holding a handkerchief full of cut paper.

THE BEGINNING

Con game nets 3 women

★ ★ ★   ★ ★ ★ *8/1972*

Detectives watched while suspects worked

Three Manhattan women were arraigned on charges of grand larceny yesterday after they swindled a Jamaica woman out of $1,500 in a confidence game, police said.

The women, Patricia Jackson, 25, Winomina Stamper, 22, and Queshawn Andre, 21, were under police surveillance for over three hours as they played their trick.

Detective Ted Rarace and Andrew Camera of the 16th District Burglary Squad and Detective George Bartlett of the Pickpocket and Confidence Squad said they saw Miss Jackson and Miss Stamper approach a woman, whose identity was withheld by police, at Union Hall St. and Archer Ave. in Jamaica yesterday afternoon and told her about finding a large sum of money.

They offered to split the money with the woman if, as a token of good faith, she would go to her bank and withdraw the $1,500 in her savings account and deposit it with the rest of the money that was found. The woman took a bus to Springfield Gardens, withdrew the money, and returned to Jamaica accompanied by Miss Jackson and Miss Stamper, police said.

There followed a brief rendezvous with the third woman, Miss Andre, in a Jamaica restaurant, a quick shuffling of money envelopes and the swindled woman was left with an envelope which she thought contained a large sum of money to be brought to a lawyer's office in the Jamaica Savings Bnkbuilding for clearance.

Meanwhile, the three suspects took off down Jamaica Avenue with the envelope containing the swindled woman's $1,500, police said. However, they were all arrested by the three detectives who had been following the whole thing.

The money was recovered but even when told by police she had been gypped, the swindled woman refused to acknowledge her part in the "scheme" until the detectives took her envelope, tore it opn and showed her the blank paper inside.

Police said it was very unusual to recover the money in such confidence ploys since it involves too much time and manpower. However, the Jamaica area has been hard hit with confidence people recently and an $250,000 has been lost this summer so far.

CHAPTER 1
INTELLIGENCE GATHERING AND THE BIRTH
OF BACKSTAGE & SOFT-SHOES

CHAPTER 5
A SURVEILLANCE PAYS OFF

Cops offer salve for 'sting' —nab '100G-a-month ring'

Packets of money and other items used in the con game are examined by Lt. Ronald Fenrich, left, and Detective Ted Farace

By STAN TRYBULSKI

The trio of bewigged and bedecked young ladies stepped out of their Corona apartment building, right into the arms of the law.

Minutes after the women were arrested yesterday by the Queens Burglary Squad, a dapper, 64-year-old man strolled through the same portals and also was arrested, smashing what police described as $100,000-a-month con game that preyed on elderly women.

The gang, which included three others arrested earlier this week, reportedly operated on a citywide basis, using the "pocketbook drop," also known as the "handkerchief switch," with a phony wad of money called a "Michigan bankroll," police said.

According to Lt. Ronald Fenrich, burglary squad commander, the demure defendants were Libby Miller, 22; Brenda Thompson, 22, and Dorothy Saunders, 24, all of Surace North Apartments, 112-22 37th Ave.

Police said the alleged ringleader was Barry Smith, 64, dressed in an expensive gray sharkskin suit, gray fedora hat, and patent leather shoes.

All four are to be arraigned today
(Turn to Page 25)

(PRESS) 7/18/75

CHAPTER 5

A SURVEILLANCE PAYS OFF (CONTINUED)

SALVE FOR THE 'STING'

★   ★   ★   ★   ★   ★

Nab 100G-a-month con ring : Cops

(Continued from Page 1)

in Kew Gardens Criminal Court on grand larceny charges, police said.

In addition, Miller is wanted by Bronx police and Thompson in Manhattan, police said.

Arrested earlier this week and arraigned on grand larceny charges, police said, were Betty Anderson, 25, Lemon Bruton, 50, and Homer Bozier, all of the Surace North address.

* * *

ACCORDING TO FENRICH, after the ring duped an elderly victim out of her savings, they might return, pose as detectives and con her a second time.

He gave the following description of the gang's alleged operation:

One of the young ladies would approach an elderly person on a Queens street and say she had found a canvas bag with a lot of money in it, then offer to share it with her intended victim.

A note found on Ms. Miller, police said, stated: "Well, Sweet Molly came through this time for $37,000. Take money and put it in Swiss account. The IRS is looking for me. See you when this thing blows over."

The note would be shown to the victim in order to lend authenticity to the story of the newly-found lost money. Then another attractive young lady, an accomplice, would show up and volunteer that she worked for a lawyer and offer to consult her boss.

A FEW MINUTES later, she would return and state that the lawyer suggested that each of the three women put up "good faith" money in an envelope until the alleged $37,000 could be divided, and the lawyer would hold the envelope.

The two young women would then accompany their victim to the bank or home, where she would get her "good faith" money and place it in the envelope, which she sealed.

Then, the envelope would be switched

and another envelope with the "Michigan roll" — play money with a real $20 bill on top and bottom. Later, the victim would discover she had been bilked.

On a few occasions, Fenrich said, the suspects use a variation, where a member of the gang would show up at the victim's home in the evening, flash a phony shield and say he was a detective.

The "detective" would tell the victim that she must have been cheated by a bank teller and ask the victim's co-operation in trapping the teller.

The next day, the victim would go to the same teller at the bank, withdraw several thousand dollars and give it to the "detective" outside, who would mark the money, then go inside to supposedly arrest the teller. Instead, he would dash out another exit, leaving his victim.

CHAPTER 6
AWARENESS AND TRAINING

Con game victim helps cops catch 2 suspects

7/5/75
Press

The courage of a 50-year old Rochdale Village woman, who had lost $2,000 in a con game known as the "handkerchief switch," and the "comeback," led to the arrest of two of the four men who police say staged the caper.

Police said the woman, whom they would not identify, was approached on a Rochdale Village street on Aug. 22 by a man who said he was a "seaman" looking for a certain address.

While the two were talking, a second man joined the conversation and the "seaman" flashed what appeared to be a large roll of bills.

The "seaman" said he didn't trust banks and did not have a bank account. The woman told him his fears were groundless and withdrew $2,000 to prove the banks were reliable.

The "seaman" said he was impressed by the woman's honesty and asked her to hold his money along with hers in a handkerchief while he and the second man went to pick up his luggage.

* * *

ONCE THE woman's money was in the handkerchief, the "switch" was made. The two men then took off with the real money, leaving the victim with a handkerchief filled with paper.

Detectives Andrew Camera and Theodore Farace of the Confidence Team of the Queens Burglarly Squad, under the direction of Lt. Ronald Fenrich, interviewed the victim and warned her of the "comeback" angle.

The "comeback" uses two different men who claim to be detectives and approach the same victim usually several days after the original incident. They generally say the original con men have been arrested and that the

victim will get her money back and a reward from the bank as well.

They say a bank teller is involved and in order to trap him the victim is given an envelope. They ask the victim to withdraw the rest of the money so the teller's fingerprints are on the envelope.

* * *

WHEN JOHN McConico, 49, of Manhattan and Percy Harris, 31, of the Bronx showed up on Sept. 2, the Rochdale Village woman was prepared.

The men claimed to be detectives from the Knapp Commission and told her the same type story Detectives Camera and Farace had warned against.

Instead of driving to her bank, however, the woman drove up to the 113th Precinct stationhouse. She was about to enter the stationhouse driveway when one of the men jammed on the brakes and threw her from the car. The two fled on foot.

She screamed and Police Officer Richard Murphy raced from the stationhouse and gave chase. Several neighborhood youths and adults pounced on McConico and held him for Murphy. The second man, although beaten by the crowd, made his getaway.

Camera and Farace re-entered the case and yesterday arrested Harris.

The investigation is continuing as detectives continue to look for the "seaman" and his companion.

129

CHAPTER 8
(DRAG) SOLO PLAYER

Santucci Reports New Wrinkle On Old Con Game

12/29/ RIDGEWOOD Time

Queens District Attorney John J Santucci today announced the indictment of a Bronx man and woman on charges of employing a new variation of the old "pocketbook drop" confidence scheme to hoodwink a 65-year-old Queens woman of $20,000 in cash from her savings and $5,000 worth of jewelry.

Santucci said the charges describe a new wrinkle on the old con game – limiting face-to-face contact with the victim to only one member of the con artist team; the standard practice for the scheme is victim contact with two people supposedly strangers to each other.

The DA said the indictment obtained by his office names as defendants Larry Ogeltree, 38, of 2332 Tiebout Ave. Bronx. and Pamela Perez, a/k/a Joan Tilson, 22, of 2185 Grand Concourse, Bronx. Both are charged with Grand Larceny, Second Degree. Each could face up to 7 years in prison if convicted. The defendants were arraigned before Justice Thomas S Agresta in Queens Supreme Court, Kew Gardens, and were paroled. A trial date is to be set in January, 1978.

The investigation leading to their arrests was conducted by

widow withdraw savings of her own to show "good faith" toward an eventual split of the found money. The victim withdrew $20,000 from four separate accounts and jewelry from her bank.

The widow gave her money and jewels to the ye give to a "mes and non-existen "attorney" to Eventually the two canvas bag woman who sa the victim's valuables and th the victim's sha The bags wer victim's safety the widow beca a check on th showed the m play cash

Detectives i investigative across the n bread", a deve probers to kee apartment of Photos taken o address led to one visitor as th who had told finding the "money." Furt led detectives t Pamela Perez

Couple Face Hearing In Swindle of Widow

1977

A Bronx couple face a court hearing Jan. 6 on charges of employing a new variation of the old "pocketbook drop" confidence scheme to hoodwink a 65-year-old Queens widow of $25,000 in cash and jewelry, Queens District Attorney John Santucci announced.

Larry Ogeltree, 38, of 2332 Tiebout Ave. and Pamela Perez, 2185 Grand Concourse, were arraigned in Queens Supreme Court before Justice Thomas Agresta after being indicted Friday by a Queens grand jury for second degree grand larceny.

Unseen Silent Partner

Santucci said the charges describe a new wrinkle on an old game—limiting face-to-face contact with the victim to only one member of the con artist team; the standard practice for the scheme is victim contact with two people supposedly strangers to each other.

Santucci said that last June, the widow was approached by a young woman who said she had found a canvas bank bag containing money.

A quick count of the phony bankroll suggested the bag contained $70,000 in cash. The widow and the woman then went to the elderly woman's home where the stranger called an "attorney" she knew for advice.

"Good Faith" Withdrawal

The advice, according to Santucci, was to have the widow withdraw $20,000 in savings from four separate bank accounts as a sign of "good faith" toward an eventual split of the found money. The widow added $5,000 worth

Eventually, the widow was given two canvas bags by the younger woman, who said one contained the victim's money and the other the share of the found $70,000.

The bags, which were deposited in the widow's safety deposit box, actually contained bogus bills, a fact the victim learned by checking the bags at a later date.

Nickname Leads to Photo

The case was investigated by the Queens burglary squad and the DA's rackets squad. In the course of the case, Santucci, said, detective came across the nickname "Shortbread," which led probers to keep a watch on the apartment of Larry Ogeltree.

A woman who visited Ogeltree was photographed and identified as the younger woman who had told the widow about finding the bag of "money." She was later identified as Miss Perez.

The two were arrested in early November and $3,000 worth of the widow's jewelry was recovered at Miss Perez' apartment, Santucci said.

The DA said that most victims of con games don't report it to police

---

9/28/77

2 indicted in 25G swindle

By EDWARD KULIK

A Bronx couple have been indicted on charges of swindling an elderly Queens woman out of $25,000 in cash and jewelry through the use of a new wrinkle in an old confidence game.

The new wrinkle, according to Queens District Attorney John J. Santucci, limits face-to-face contact with the victim to only one member of the con artist team, instead of the usual two. He warned that this variation of the old "pocketbook drop" has been spreading throughout the

city in the last several months.

The indictment, the DA said, states that on June 23 a 65-year-old widow was approached by a younger woman who said she had found a canvas bank bag containing what appeared to be about $70,000 in cash.

The two then went to the widow's home where the stranger called an "attorney" she knew "for advice." His advice included having the widow withdraw her life savings to show "good faith" toward an eventual split of the found money. The widow withdrew $20,000 cash plus

jewelry from a safety deposit box.

The widow gave the money and jewels to the younger woman to give to a "messenger" who would deliver it to the "attorney" to make a record.

Later, the widow was given two canvas bags, one supposedly containing the victim's own money and jewels, the other her share of the $70,000, and both bags were placed in the widow's safety deposit box.

The widow eventually became suspicious, checked the bags' contents, and found only play money.

A lengthy investigation by Detectives Andrew Camera, Theodore Farace and Anthony Tempesta, aided by Asst. DA Richard Brook, led to the arrests early this month of Larry Ogeltree, 22, of 2332 Tiebout Av., and Pamela Perez, a/k/a Joan Tilson, 22, of 2185, both of The Bronx.

Each was charged with grand larceny, second degree, and could face up to seven years in state prison if convicted. A trial date will be set next month.

Police said about $3000-worth of the victim's jewelry was recovered.

CHAPTER 9
THE GYPSY SWINDLE

3 Gypsies Seized as Knock-on-Door Robbers

DAILY NEWS, WEDNESDAY, DECEMBER 21, 1977

By JACK LEAHY

Three gypsies, including a 16-year-old girl, were arrested yesterday in Richmond Hill as suspects in a series of robberies that terrorized senior citizens in Queens, Brooklyn and Westchester, police said.

The three tricked their way into the homes of their likely victims by posing as utility workers, according to Detective Richard Nicastro, who led the three to a gypsy team.

None of the incidents where losses totaled more than $5,000 was inflicted in the suspects were seriously injured in the victims said.

The suspects were identified as Jim Danis, 37, of 933 E. 2nd St., Brooklyn, and Vera Pireska, 16,

Stokes, 25, who lives with the girl at 41-16 29th Ave. Astoria, and Tina Camera, who his performed them knocking on doors near South Conduit Ave. and 145th St.

"They were told to be on the look-out for," said Camera, who was an unmarked car.

"Their M.O. [method of operation] it is fit the area with Piraca in an unmarked car.

"Their M.O. [method of operation] it was to keep knocking on doors until they found an elderly person living alone," he said.

"If someone answered the door and looked like they just moved on, gypsies self, they said they were at the door."

Reports coming in from Astoria, Flushing, Corona, and Richmond Hill have been steadily clothing and fitting over the past three months, police said.

The suspects' description occurred in the Olinville, Flushing, Ridge and Westchester, according to

CHAPTER 10
BARBARA ST. JAMES
INVESTIGATION

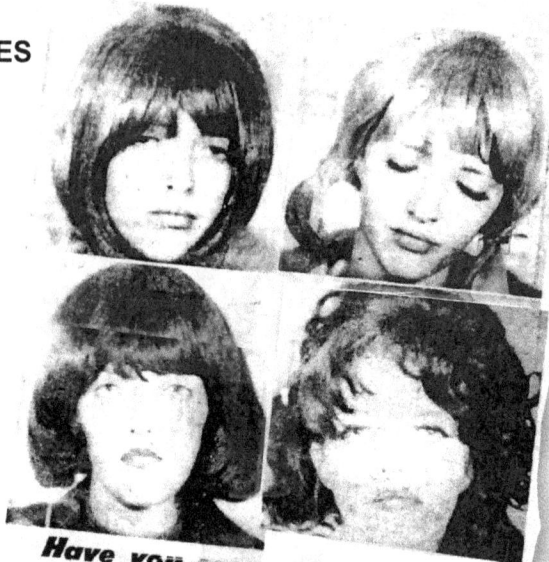

Have you seen this woman?
Appearances can deceive, as these four photos of same woman attest.

2XQ 3/17/78 - NEWS DAILY NEWS, FR

Lineup Bills Her As 90G Con Girl

By WILLIAM BUTLER

A 5-foot 1, 115-pound former go-go dancer is expected to tread the runway once again at Manhattan Police Headquarters today, but the audience will be composed of victims of more than $150,000 in con games from throughout the metropolitan area.

Police called for a lineup starring Randee Brodsky, 20, who allegedly gave up a $300-a-week career as a dancer in midtown Manhattan bars in favor of working a con game that apparently paid vastly more.

Queens District Attorney John Santucci said yesterday that the dancer had been arrested and held without bail on charges involving more than $90,000 and was under suspicion in gyps involving almost $60,000 more.

"Found Money" Game

He said Miss Brodsky practiced the old "found money" scam on elderly women in Jackson Heights, Forest Hills, Manhattan, White Plains and Fort Lee, N.J.

The case broke open when Miss Brodsky was arrested late Wednesday at Kennedy Airport as she got off a return flight from Acapulco. She was seized by agents of the district attorney's office, Queens Burglary Squad Detectives Theodore Forace and Andrew Camera and Port Authority Police Officers John Morrow and Joseph Butler.

She was arrested on warrants accus-

ing her of failing to appear in Kew Gardens Criminal Court last October after having been arrested for an attempted con game in Jackson Heights and a successful operation in Forest Hills that cost a 60-year-old woman the proceeds of her $320 Social Security check.

Another warrant, issued by Fort Lee authorities, accused her of cheating another 60-year-old woman of $30,000 in savings. Manhattan authorities named her in a $52,000 score, and White Plains cited one for $10,000.

Other Cases Turned Up

Santucci said the attractive woman pretended to find money in a pocketbook on the street, offered to share it with a targeted elderly woman passing by and persuading the victim to withdraw savings as a sign of good faith.

During the hunt for Brodsky after she failed to appear in court on the Queens cases, her connection with cases throughout the metropolitan area were discovered, Santucci said.

Police said she gave her address as 215 E. 64th St., New York.

BACKSTAGE AND SOFT-SHOES PHOTOGRAPHS

CHAPTER 12

CONCLUSION

It was a tough decision to leave the Pickpocket Confidence Squad after a successful career working on known confidence games for over seven years. Backstage and Soft-Shoes left a mark in the minds of confidence operators working in the New York City area. Our street names were still known 12 years later when I was working in Corporate Security in Lower Manhattan. One day in 1999, 12 years after my retirement, I was getting my shoes shined on Pine Street around noon. The streets at that time were full of people getting lunch and shopping. While sitting in the chair, I noticed three males in conversation right outside the store. I immediately recognized this as the Stuff Handkerchief Switch confidence game that was in progress. I got up with only one shoe shinned, went outside, and interrupted the conversation. I joined in and began a dialogue of offering my help. Both male subjects did not know what to say. When I identified myself as Backstage and both men immediately recognized the name by the expressions on their faces. One stated "I thought you retired". I replied, "Backstage and Soft-Shoes never retire". I told the two men this was their lucky day and to walk away. One of the men stated, "Thank you, Mr. Backstage" as they walked away. No police were in the area at the time. As a civilian it would have been difficult to try holding two subjects and the victim, who at this point had no idea what was going on. I spent minutes informing the victim of what they said and how those men would try to steal his money. The gentlemen thanked me and left a little bit wiser. I went back into the store and finished getting my other shoe shinned.

The Informant
It was agreed that our Informant Judith would be released from the Nassau County Jail with the understanding that she was being released into my custody to cooperate with me for a one-year period. After one year she was required to surrender to both the Georgia and Florida authorities to face charges in those states that were pending.

In early 1978. I was in contact with the prosecutor and detective assigned on the Georgia case and discussed the assistance Judith had given Andy and I over the past year. They agreed to follow whatever the Florida authorities decide to do upon sentencing. She had agreed to plead guilty to all the charges in both states one year earlier. I then contacted the detective in the Broward County Sheriff's office and informed him that Judith was flying down to Florida to surrender personally to him. I told the detective there was no need to send me his paycheck (the bet we made one year earlier). The key was the success she gave the Queens Confidence Team, which was more important to Andy and me not to take his paycheck. Thanks were given for his help in allowing Judith to get out of jail under my control. The day before Judith was to fly down to Florida, I met her for the last time in person. Judith assured me she would be on the flight to Florida as promised and was hoping for the best on her cases. Nothing was promised to her one year earlier only the opportunity to offer to the court her cooperation and show the results for consideration upon sentencing.

I received a phone call from the detective in the Broward County Sheriff's office who informed me that Judith did in fact show up at his office and surrendered. He was still in shock that she did not con me or Andy. She had lived up to her word, now it was time for me to do the same.

A court date in Florida was set for Judith to plead guilty to the two outstanding fraud cases against her in Broward County. I flew down to Florida and testified on her behalf. At the hearing, I took the stand and related all the arrests Andy and I had made because of her cooperation. The Queens District Attorney had given his endorsement of the success we achieved based on her information, which was offered to the Judge at this hearing. Her information led to high-profile cases being solved and as a result other crimes were also solved. Both the Queens DA and Nassau DA agreed on the decision on sentencing by the Florida court. After I gave testimony based on all her cooperation; the Judge decided to give her probation with a stipulation, she had to sign into a drug rehabilitation program as part of his sentencing. The Georgia authorities were informed of the judge's decision of probation and agreed to close their case. Judith relocated to another state and did in fact sign into a drug rehabilitation program, as so ordered by the court. This was the right thing to do, helping someone who gives up a life of crime and to get back to a normal life. It was a good feeling for both of us that we were able to help Judith.

In May of 2024, I received a phone call from a female who identified herself as Judith, having no idea who that was. When Judith gave her last name, I almost fell off my chair. It had been close to 50 years since we spoke. Judith and her partner agreed to meet my wife and I for dinner. Our dinner together and the connection after all this time was really the driving factor for me to complete the book that Andy and I started 50 years earlier.

Now it was time to locate Andy, a.k.a. Soft-Shoes. I had not spoken with him for over 30 years, since I was working in Corporate Security in Manhattan. After searching the internet and personal databases, Andy was located. He was now retired and living in Florida. After a long phone call to reconnect, we decided to meet in person and to complete the book we started to write close to 50 years ago. I flew down to Florida to finally meet with my old partner in crime, Soft-Shoes.

Present Day

In the 70's, a nationwide association was formed with active members of law enforcement who investigated confidence games as participants, The National Association of Bunco Investigators (NABI). This organization tracks various confidence games and other swindles across the country. Its mission, to keep its membership up to date on what is occurring in other states in the hope of the information shared, will help solve other cases. Across our country, confidence games are occurring daily, most recently in 2024 four subjects, two males and two females were arrested in Maryland pulling off the Pigeon Dorp (Drag) or Pocketbook Drop for $40,000. Today the New York City Police Department is now focusing on major financial frauds, Bit Coin, Ponzi swindles and others. The Squad has detectives assigned to transnational groups, such as the Gypsies to investigate on a city-wide basis. Known street confidence games are left to the local detective squads to investigate like it was back in 1972. The Financial Frauds Unit still maintains a photo file of known street confidence operators arrested in the past to assist in investigations being conducted at a local level. Victims can view the photos at that unit and if someone is identified, the investigation is then left to the local area detective to try to solve. Specialization was dissolved years ago, and borough wide statistics, unfortunately today are not kept on street confidence games.

NEWS ARTICLE PUBLISHED OCTOBER 31, 2024*

CRIME & COURTS

Four Suspects Arrested For "Pigeon Drop" Scam; Additional Victims Possible

by Prince George's County Police Department
October 31, 2024

Kenneth Gooden, James Davis, Mary Daniel, and Connie Williams

*Published by Baynet online news and entertainment

UPPER MARLBORO, Md. – The PGPD's Financial Crimes Unit identified four suspects who targeted an elderly woman last week in a "pigeon drop" scam in the county. A pigeon drop scam involves convincing a victim to give the suspect(s) a large amount of cash as collateral with the hope of then sharing a sum of money.

The suspects are 77-year-old James Davis of Birmingham, Alabama, 64-year-old Connie Williams of Birmingham, Alabama, 59-year-old Mary Daniel of Antioch, Tennessee, and 36-year-old Kenneth Gooden of Birmingham, Alabama. They are charged with stealing tens of thousands of dollars from the victim in District Heights. Detectives located and arrested the suspects in a shopping center in Clinton moments after approaching their next potential victim.

On October 22, 2024, the victim called 911 to report she'd been the victim of a scam. She advised detectives that on October 21, 2024, she encountered two people, a man and a woman, outside of a business in the 7700 block of Marlboro Pike. The individuals advised the victim they found a bag full of money and asked if it belonged to the victim which it did not. The suspects soon convinced the victim that instead of turning the money into police, they should donate it to charity. They then convinced the victim to withdraw money from her account so the newly withdrawn bills couldn't be traced. Over a two-day period, the victim withdrew nearly $40,000 from her account which the suspects ultimately stole.

Using various investigative techniques, Financial Crimes Unit detectives located the suspects on October 24, 2024, at a shopping center on Woodyard Road in Clinton. Two of the suspects were seen approaching another elderly woman in a parking lot. The suspects were taken into custody. Detectives believe these suspects likely targeted other victims in our county and would like for any victims who haven't done so, to please report the crime, regardless of whether the victim suffered a financial loss.

The PGPD reminds residents to never give money or financial information to anyone who you just met in person, online or on the phone. If something seems to be good to be true, it usually is.

SUMMARY

Looking back on our careers, Andy, and I both felt this was the most rewarding assignment detectives could have. We created a name for ourselves even though they were only street names, it stopped victims from losing their life savings as a result. We both disagree with other opinions about the victims on these known confidence games. Having investigated hundreds of cases, the victims who were involved were not in it for the greed but as an extension of their life. Having companionship, if only for a day or hours meant so much to a senior person. The share of found money would help them live longer and continue to be independent without seeking financial help from their family or children. Other victims who were financially sound did it out of greed.

My Confidence Team partner, Andy Camera a.k.a. Soft-Shoes left the New York City Police Department after 21 years taking an investigators position with the Special Prosecutors Office in New York. He worked in that office for one year. He decided to enter the corporate world and joined the Brooklyn Union Gas Company. During his tenure at that company, he advanced to take on the role of Coordinator of Management Development and Training for the company. He retired from the Gas Company. He now resides in Florida.

Judith, our Informant, after leaving the drug rehabilitation program, ended her life of crime. With a clean slate she raised her daughter and started a business, which she owned and managed for close to 20 years. She is now fully retired and a grandmother and lives in her home state.

As for me, "Backstage", I retired in 1987 from the NYPD after 23 years and joined the Investment Bank, J.P. Morgan as an investigator, eventually taking over the Global Security Director's position two years later. I remained there for 15 years and retired as a Managing Director of the firm. I now reside in Las Vegas and started an all-former law enforcement volunteer group right after the attack on our country on September 11, 2001. The Volunteer Homeland Reserve Unit (VHRU) had over 450 former law enforce-ment members who were considered force multipliers, assisting local police agencies in Southern Nevada. While running this volunteer organization, I formed a boutique security company that I managed for 15 years, providing security services to the Wynn-Encore hotel and others. I now own and manage a training academy, The Nevada Security

Guard Training Academy (NSGTA) for Security Officers. In addition, to keep busy, I started a non-profit corporation, called Flags for Nevada, installing American Flags on homes as a sign of patriotism.

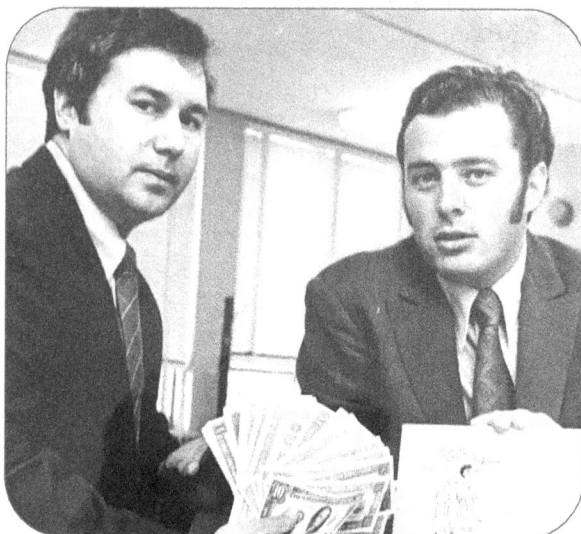

Detective Andy Camera (left) and Detective Ted Farace
holding a Michigan Bank Roll.

Ted and Andy present day.

BACKSTAGE AND SHOFT-SHOES

Detective Ted Farace went by his street name "Backstage" for his behind-the-scenes mastery of complex cases. He joined the NYPD as a police officer. His tenacious skill and commitment were soon recognized with promotions to Detective Third Grade and later to Detective Second Grade. Following his retirement in 1987, Detective Farace embarked on a new chapter, taking on a key role as a director of security in the corporate sector, where he ensured the protection of assets and personnel with the same vigilance and dedication he displayed on the streets of New York. He now resides in Las Vegas owning and managing a security guard training academy. He also owns and manages a non-profit organization that installs American flags on homes as a gesture of patriotism.

Detective Andy Camera known as "Soft-Shoes" had a quiet yet effective approach. He began his career with the NYPD as a police officer. Over the years, his dedication and sharp investigative skills earned him promotions to Detective Third Grade and then to Detective Second Grade.

After years of honorable service on the force, Detective Camera retired in 1981. However, his journey didn't end there. He seamlessly transitioned into the corporate world, where he leveraged his law enforcement expertise to become a successful coordinator of management training at the Brooklyn Union Gas Company, guiding future leaders with the same precision he applied in his police work. Andy is now retired and resides in Florida.